BEYOND THE BREAD

TASTEFUL EXPLORATION WITH JAM & MARMALADE

CHRISTOPHER WILSON
WITH IMAGES BY KASHA BIALAS
INTRODUCTION BY ELIZABETH SEGRAN

LUNAGROWN PUBLISHING

A DIVISION OF LUNAGROWN

WWW.LUNAGROWN.COM

PRINTED IN THE UNITED STATES OF AMERICA

COPYRIGHT

Published By
LunaGrown Publishing
PO Box 621, Cuddebackville NY, 12729

Printed and bound
Chester Printing
Middletown, New York USA

Library of Congress Control Number: 2017908701

ISBN 978-0-692-90081-9
First Edition
10 9 8 7 6 5 4 3 2 1

www.lunagrown.com

LunaGrown

ABOUT THE AUTHOR

Christopher is the owner/operator of LunaGrown Jam, which began as a home based business in 2012. LunaGrown currently operates a commercial kitchen on a small berry farm and vineyard in the Hudson Valley of New York. All Lunagrown products still utilize small batch production.

Christopher began his early career in visual merchandising before seeking employment in the bar and restaurant industry. This field offered hands on experience in both the front and back end of the restaurant/bar business. With his focus on management and culinary art he refined his skills.

He has Master Food Preservation Certification from Cornell Cooperative Extension and is working to acquire his Better Process Control Certification from the University of California.

He is a retired singer/songwriter with numerous recordings released. Christopher is an avid reader and also enjoys his time outdoors, hiking or tending the fields. His spare time is focused on agricultural studies, website development and his dogs.

ABOUT THIS BOOK

When I began LunaGrown Jam, I was surprised at the number of times I heard "Oh, I have so much jam at home." or in the case of Green Tomato Jam "What would you do with that?" I assumed that people opened a jar of jam and finished it in about a month, if not sooner, depending on the number of jam lovers in their household.

In the case of the Green Tomato Jam and other more regional favorites, I honestly thought people were more explorative. I thought everyone just considered the endless possibilities food offered.

I learned that some people were cautious with food exploration. Jam as a salad dressing sounded a bit odd to me, until I considered the salad it would be accompanying. Then perhaps it didn't sound as odd, but more intriguing.

As LunaGrown grew I wanted to let people know that they could enjoy jam and marmalade in ways that went beyond a spoonful on some hot buttered bread. Really though, fresh butter and jam on warm homemade bread is a challenge to beat.

This book offers some of my favorite recipes utilizing jam and marmalade. While all recipes have been tested with LunaGrown Jam and I would love for you to become a LunaGrown fan, these recipes do not rely on LunaGrown to be enjoyable. You will do best with a high quality product though. If you have a favorite by all means give it a try!

Go beyond the morning toast with these delicious things.

"Keep in mind that your goal is to offer tastes that compliment one another, not over power one another. It should be a thoughtful and sophisticated adventure for your palate, not a college frat party for your mouth. "

~ *The Jam Maker, LunaGrown*

TABLE OF CONTENTS

DINNER CONTINUED:

DESSERTS　　88

COOKIES　　120

ADDITIONAL IDEAS　　133
QUICK REFERENCE IDEAS　　137

INTRODUCTION

When I was seven years old, my family lived in France. That summer, I went strawberry picking for the first time in my life. I have very clear memories of going out into the patches at a farm, my fingers red and sticky, eating my fill of ripe, sweet berries.

That evening, when we were home, my mother made an enormous vat of strawberry jam. The kitchen counter filled up with neat rows of glass jars, filled with hot, red jam. Nearly three decades on, the taste of strawberry jam still transports me back to that day: I vividly remember the sun on the back of my neck, my belly full, and the feeling of contentment.

Jam has that effect. It's an emotional food. We eat it when we need comfort, or when we need a little boost at the start of our day.

This is something that Christopher knows well. I met him several years ago, when I was just starting my career as a journalist. At the time, I had a blog about my own experiments with jam, and Chris reached out to me.

Over the years, we've written back and forth to each other between Cuddebackville in upstate New York where he is based, and Cambridge, Massachusetts where I live. We've sent each other Christmas presents and talked about the goings on in each others' lives. I love hearing about his dogs and he gets regular updates about my toddler's latest antics. (LunaGrown was the first jam she tasted when she was all of 11 months old. Chris had included a tiny spoon in his holiday shipment so she could partake in it.)

I have tasted gallons of his delicious jams in a wide array of flavors. What sets his jam apart is that he recognizes that jam is much more than a preserved fruit with sugar. Jam can be sacred, because it contains memories.

In his case, it also contains dreams. I've watched Chris grow his business from a small operation based in his kitchen to an impressive, blossoming company that ships around the country. Chris is constantly pushing the boundaries of his own creativity when it comes to developing new recipes. But he also believes that jam can be enjoyed in creative ways.

I generally think of jam as a breakfast food, something I throw on my bread or yogurt. But as Chris demonstrates in this book, jam can be incorporated into many drinks and foods, and paired with things you might not expect, like salad and beer. Among my favorite dishes on this list are the sautéed carrots and parsnips with apricot jam, and the coconut bread with lime marmalade. I'm sure that as you work through the many recipes Chris has thought up, you'll find the ones that you come back to time and again.

This book inspires us to think about jam in new ways. It can add a little magic to just about any meal.

Elizabeth Segran
Staff Writer, Fast Company Magazine

ENTERTAINING
A GUIDE TO PAIRING

SUGGESTED JAM AND CHEESE PAIRINGS

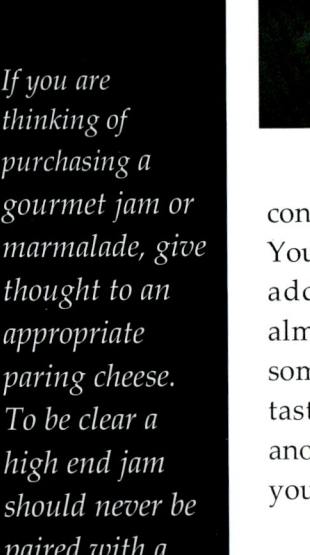

If you are thinking of purchasing a gourmet jam or marmalade, give thought to an appropriate paring cheese. To be clear a high end jam should never be paired with a cheese that cost less than the jar of jam or marmalade.

When pairing cheese and jam, look at the whole picture, consider all the possibilities before deciding on a limited few. You may be serving your cheese and jam pairings with wine, additional fruits, and maybe black walnuts or smoked almonds, an artisan bread and fresh basil or ginger. But, sometimes, less is more. Keep in mind that your goal is to offer tastes that complement one another, not over power one another. It should be a thoughtful, sophisticated adventure for your palate, not a college frat party for your mouth.

Serve your cheese alongside its accompaniment rather than mixed together. Jam should not be poured over the top of your cheese. You and your guests should be able to enjoy the cheese by itself, as well as the jam, then enjoy them together in a combination that suits their personal tastes. Offering additional accompaniments is welcome, but choose wisely. Remember, your goal is sophistication.

Choose a few key items that support the nuances of your cheese and jam will ensure a memorable experience.

Acquiring the highest quality cheese is an important part of the process. Once you have chosen the cheese upon which to build your paring, it is imperative to engage it with a discerning jam.

A sophisticated cheese paired with LunaGrown distinguished Jam is certain to bring you great pleasure.

If you are not a wine connoisseur ask questions and find out what wines would best suit the pairing you had in mind as well as the atmosphere you are creating.

When serving jam and cheese as a pairing it is best to chill your jam as well as the serving dish or cup the jam will go into, this will keep the jam firm for a longer period of time while it sets out as well as keeping it fresh in appearance and flavor.

SUGGESTED CHEESE PAIRINGS

Apple Jam - *Mozzarella, Goat, Fontina, or English Cheddar, Gran Padano*

Apricot Jam, - *Parmagiano Reggianno, Gran Padano, Monterey Dry Jack, Gran Queso*

Blackberry Jam - *Stilton Blue, Manchego, Triple Crème, Camembert , Goat or Feta*

Blueberry Jam - *Goat, Stilton or Manchego*

Cranberry Jam - *Goat, Camembert, Triple Crème or Brie*

Fig Jam - *Brie, Boursin, Mascarpone, Mozzarella, Red hawk Cheese*

Hot Pepper Jelly - *Brie, Triple Crème , Sharp Cheddar, Colby*

Mixed Berry Jam - *Aged Asiago, Dry Monterey Jack, Goat, Stilton*

Peach Jam - *Goat, Stronger Blues, Baked Brie*

Pear Jam - *Gorgonzola , Brie , Stilton or Triple Crème*

Plum Jam - *Goat, Triple Crème, Smoked Gouda*

Raspberry Jam - *Parmigiano-Reggiano, Brie, Triple Crème*

Tomato Jam (green) - *Aged Gorgonzola, Brie, Jarlsberg, Roquefort, Stilton*

Tomato Jam (red) - *Gorgonzola Dolce (sweet), Muenster, Brie*

Strawberry Jam - *Goat, Triple Crème, or Brie*

Country Traditional Jams – *Huckleberry, Elderberry, Wild Grape are best served with an Extra Sharp Cheddar, or a Muenster*

Bold flavored cheeses pair well with strong flavored jams. The opposite is also true: mild cheeses unite well with subtly flavored jams. Be aware, when pairing to avoid domination of one flavor over the other. Your goal is to achieve the magic that happens when good flavors complement each other.

PAIRING JAM AND WINE

Suggestions on pairing wine and jam are pretty straight forward, thankfully, because this is a very important part of pulling your affair together. How can one have cheese without wine, especially if you are going the extra step to pair it with the right Jam?

Pairing your jam with wine can sometimes be a bit tricky, but the process is made easier by familiarizing yourself with the type and brand of wine you are planning to enjoy. It is also beneficial to know the region in which the wine was grown, as this will affect the fragrance or subtleties of the wine itself and how it will taste when paired with your chosen jam.

For instance, your Pinot Grigio/Pinot Gris can come from many different places, from France or Italy, from Oregon or California, and can offer different flavor nuances.

Your Chardonnay, depending on where it's grown and how it's processed, can taste semi-sweet or sour, heady or light. Its distinction can range from apple, tangerine, lemon, lime, melon, to oak and anywhere in-between.

If your wine has a subtle blackberry flavor then it would be best paired with a jam from the berry category. If your wine has a slight hint of apple or pear, then one of these jams would best enhance that slight fragrance for an intensified flavor experience.

The goal in pairing your wine and jam is to connect the subtle undertones of the wine with that of your jam and then match the cheese that brings it all together. Below is a list of suggested wine and jam pairings. However, knowing your wine will help you choose the best flavor combination.

THE REDS

- Cabernet Sauvignon – Black Currant Jam, Blackberry Jam
- Italian Chianti – Red or Green Tomato Jam
- Merlot – Plum Jam, Cherry Jam, Cranberry Jams
- Pinot Noir – Rica Barreja Jam, Pear or Apple Jam, Strawberry Jam
- Sangiovese – Blueberry Jam, Cherry or Fig Jam
- Zinfandel – Apricot Jam, Peach Jam, Plum Jam

THE WHITES

- Chardonnay -Apple Jam, Lemon or Orange Marmalade
- Pinot Grigio/Pinot Gris – Raspberry or Cranberry Jam, Apricot or Peach Jam
- Riesling – Pear Jam or Marmalade, Pineapple or Apricot Jam

BLUSH WINES

- White Zinfandel – Raspberry Jam, Peach or Apricot Jam
- White Merlot – Blackberry or Blueberry Jam
- White Grenache – Strawberry Jam, Cherry Jam

It is best to be well acquainted with the flavor nuances of the wine you have chosen to serve. The flavor undertones of the wine will be of assistance in creating the most memorable pairing.

CORRECTLY PAIRING JAM AND BEER, THAT'S BOLD!

Pairing beer with most foods requires an understanding of the flavor profiles presented in your beverage. As always, general idea of your meal plan or cheese selection will also help you choose the jam that will best complement your favorite brew.

For example, a crisp beer such as a cream ale or a wheat ale might have background notes of pears or summer berries. In this case, a pear or berry jam would enhance those flavors. From here, you would choose a cheese or food accompaniment appropriate to the setting.

If you have chosen your food course first and are serving a rich meal of roast beef with plum jam dressing, a strong, hearty ale would be a suitable beer choice.

A general rule to follow when pairing jam and beer is to enhance the nuances present in your beverage. Choose jams or marmalades that won't compete with or upstage lighter-flavored beverages, and choose darker, more flavorful fruit preserves to pair with heartier beers, stronger cheeses or richer foods.

With such increased diversity in brew masters styles and beverage choices, it is important to know your beer's characteristics. If you are uncertain, ask questions! These suggested pairings are guidelines for your enjoyment.

If you are creating a cheese and beer pairing it is best to be mindful that neither the beer nor the cheese like to be exposed to oxygen for any length of time. Cut cheeses as you are serving them, and open beers as you are serving them. Some cheeses and beers are best served at room temperature to achieve the height of flavor. Jam however should be served chilled. If you are serving jam in an open dish, it is best to chill the dish prior to presentation.

PAIRING BEER & JAM: SUGGESTIONS

Some attempt to find similar traits when pairing beer with jam. The idea is that there is a pleasant echo. Notes in one sip evoke flavors in past or future bites. The opposite approach infers that contrasting flavors are pleasing, that they may give rise to one another's flavor profile.

- **Spicy Blue Cheese ~ *Wild Ale* ~ Black or Red Currant Jam**

- **Feta or Goat Cheese ~ *Hefeweizen* ~ Strawberry Jam**

- **Camembert or Fontina Cheese ~ *American Wheat Ale* ~ Blueberry, Blackberry or Rica Barreja Jam**

- **Sharp Cheddar or Gorgonzola Cheese ~ *IPA* ~ Apple or Pear Jam**

- **Monterey Jack or Gouda Cheese ~ *Kolsch, Cream Ale, Pale Ale* ~ Lemon Marmalade, Orange Marmalade, Apricot Jam**

- **Goat or Gouda Cheese ~ *Strong Golden Ale* ~ Apricot, Golden Plum or Peach Jam**

- **Blue Cheese ~ *Amber/Red Ale* ~ Apple or Pear Jam**

- **Gruyère or Winnimere Cheese ~ *Belgian Dark Ale* ~ Cherry Jam or Orange Marmalade**

- **Goat or Smoked Gouda Cheese ~ *Old or Strong Ale* ~ Plum Jam**

- **Parmigiano-Reggiano or Feta Cheese ~ *Imperial Stout* ~ Raspberry Jam**

- **Asiago, Cheshire or Colby Cheese ~ *English Brown Ale or Bock* ~ Fig or Raisin Jam**

ARE YOUR SOCIAL GATHERINGS MEETING EXPECTATIONS?

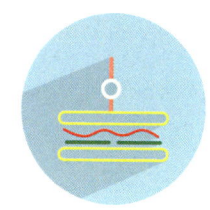

Some pointers on a clear path to a well-planned social gathering. We are not talking about a large reception by any means but a small social get-together. The same suggestions would also apply for a more intimate gathering.

One of the first things we would like to mention is that if you are serving alcoholic beverages of any type it is imperative that you also serve food. Choose an assortment of foods that complement your beverage choice as this will also help balance the alcohol consumption.

There is nothing worse than offering the finest wines or cognacs to guests who find that their palate is left empty at the end of the evening. Even worse are inebriated guests who mismanage their social skills. Offering foods that complement your beverages can assist in a well managed gathering.

Keeping in mind that this is a social gathering and not a sit-down meal, be specific in thought when choosing your menu. Offering a well balanced array of dairy, grain, protein, and fruit in addition to your beverage and, of course, jam will meet your needs perfectly.

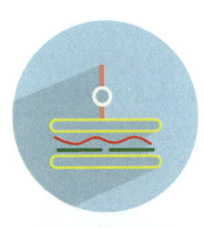

There are many cheeses and cheese nuances to choose from. Artisan breads, scones, whole grain crackers or the likes are a perfect starting point.

We suggest thinly sliced well salted meats such as Prosciutto, Salami, or Sopressata even smoked salmon or salted fish. Or if you are comfortable some finer roasted nut varieties. I always suggest jam when it comes to gatherings and pairings, fresh fruit is also important.

Fresh fruit, when serving most alcoholic beverages serves a few purposes. It can subtly enhance the flavor of the beverage and oftentimes counter any bitterness the beverage might have left behind. This is especially true with wines.

Also, fruit contains both fiber and natural sugars which tell our bodies to utilize what is in our stomachs and encourages the digestion of alcohols in the body. Brandied pears do not count as a fruit in this instance, though.

While pastries, cakes and pies are certainly festive, we don't suggest heavily sugared items for a gathering such as discussed. In our opinion, they would be better served at a celebratory event.

Chocolate however, is included here. A fine bittersweet chocolate can add an air of decadence to any social gathering. Choose your chocolate wisely, though. There are a great number of gourmet chocolates available, choose one that best suits your occasion. It is usually wise to avoid milk chocolate and opt for a dark or bittersweet instead.

Entertaining should be a fairly effortless task when done with thought and kindness. Your gathering should not be daunting but more of an adventure, or exploration of combinations that compliment one another.

SOME SUGGESTIONS

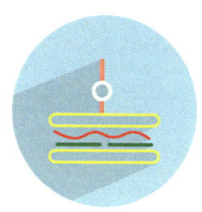

THE SOPHISTICATED INFUSION

LunaGrown Lemon Lavender Marmalade
United with a distinguished gin or vodka. A classic cheddar cheese and perhaps some light sea fare. Accompanied by some dark chocolate, artisan bread and rosemary spiced walnuts.

THE DECADENT LIAISON

LunaGrown Raspberry Jam
Tapped on a dark chocolate mint wafer or chocolate scone. We suggest a Pecorino or Gouda cheese, served with a perfect vodka martini, Up! Served with additional fruits and glazed pecans.

THE DISTINGUISHED AFFAIR

LunaGrown Wild Blueberry Jam
Coupled with a young Chianti. We suggest Blue or Asiago cheese and perhaps some thinly sliced Prosciutto. Accompanied by a savory scone, some fresh berries and dark chocolate.

THE VELVET TOUCH

LunaGrown Spiced Fig Jam
Spread on warm whole wheat pita bread. We suggest a generous portion of fresh spinach and feta cheese. served with a balsamic vinaigrette. Enjoy with a chilled blush wine, and sweet cherries

THE SPICY MORNING

LunaGrown Chipotle Hot Pepper Jelly
Atop an omelet with red and green bell peppers, bacon and yellow cherry tomatoes. Served with chive topped sour cream. Hot buttermilk biscuits and fresh seasonal fruits..

THE AUTUMN EMBRACE

LunaGrown Cranberry Jam
Accompanied by fresh pears, sourdough baguettes and sharp white NY cheddar cheese. Perhaps some warmed cider or cognac. White chocolate and spiced walnuts are a beautiful accompaniment.

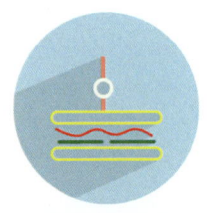

When preparing for your gathering it is important to be aware of the number of guests you are expecting. If you are expecting a larger crowd, it is better to create several smaller trays that can be chilled prior to serving, rather than one large spread (unless you can keep it iced).

This will help keep the appearance of abundance even as supplies dwindle. With careful planning, you can ensure your meats, cheeses, and jams maintain optimum temperatures for service and will avoid quick spoilage.

Swap out serving trays as needed to keep your guests enjoying the freshest delights you have to offer. Please avoid storing fresh flowers with your food offerings as it will cause early spoilage of fruits and some meats.

BEVERAGES
COOL DRINKS MADE WITH JAM

DELICIOUS SUMMER JAM DRINKS

It's summertime and it's hot! There is nothing better on a warm afternoon or evening than an icy cold beverage. Yes, there are the standard soda drinks, the sugar-laden 'juices', and other bottled concoctions, but, what about some nice homemade lemonade or iced tea? You can create an even better drink by forgoing most of the sugar while adding a unique hint of flavor with jam.

You will find these drinks easy and enjoyable. By all means, create your own signature summer cooler by altering your jam choices. This is a great way to use up the last few tablespoons of the jam in your refrigerator rather than letting it go to waste!

CUCUMBER CHIPOTLE MARTINI

- 1 tablespoon LunaGrown Chipotle Jelly
- 1 tablespoon cucumber chopped
- 5 ounces vodka
- 1 ounce cucumber syrup
- Cucumber slices as garnish

Place the Chipotle Jelly and cucumber in a blender or bullet blender. Top with ice, then pour in the cucumber syrup and vodka of choice. blend well. Pour the cocktail into a frozen martini glass, then garnish with cucumber or lime slices.

JAM MAKERS SUMMERTIME COOL DOWN

- 1 large glass of ice, pack that ice in there
- 1 tbsp LunaGrown Plum Jam
- 1 small handful assorted fresh fruit and a chocolate mint leaf (if it's growing well enough)
- Chilled water
- This needs No Sugar

Fill that glass with ice and add 1 full rounded spoonful of jam to the top. Pour in chilled water and stir. Toss fresh fruit and mint leaf on the top and grab a straw. When you hit the bottom enjoy the cool fresh fruit and ice

BLUEBERRY JAM LEMONADE

- ½ cup freshly squeezed lemon juice
- 4 tbsp LunaGrown blueberry jam, 4 1/2 cups cold water
- 1/4 cup sugar (optional)
- Ice

In a large pitcher whisk together lemon juice and blueberry jam. Pour in water and ice and store to combine. Serve cold with a large straw. Garnish with fresh berries and mint.

RASPBERRY JAM ICED TEA

- 3-4 black tea bags (boil 2 cups of water and add tea bags. Let seep for 5 minutes. Add an additional 2 cups cold water
- ¼ cup Sugar to taste (optional)
- 4 tbsp LunaGrown Raspberry Jam Garnish with Fresh Raspberries and some Mint leaves

Make tea, add sugar (optional) and jam. Allow to cool in refrigerator for 2-3 hours. Pour over ice and serve with fresh raspberries and mint leaves (serves 4)

A good marmalade combined with a tall glass of ice water makes a refreshing and rejuvenating drink on a hot afternoon. Light, subtle and relaxing, the way summer afternoons were meant to be.

PINEAPPLE PEACH JAM FRUIT SMOOTHIE

- 2 cup fresh pineapple chunks
- ½ sliced banana
- ½ cups coconut milk
- ½ cup pineapple juice
- 4 tbsp Peach Jam (or one of your favorites)
- 1-2 cups of ice
- 2 to 3 tbsp honey or to taste (optional)

In a blender add ice, coconut milk, and pineapple juice. Blend until ice is smooth. Add Jam and fruit to the mixture and blend again until a shake like consistency. If this is too thick you may add a touch of coconut milk or pineapple juice. LunaGrown recommends you taste before adding sweeteners as the flavor will change with the ripeness of the fruits you use.

Flavor combinations are endless when utilizing jam in your beverages. You are also enjoying the benefits of lower sugar, great flavor, and the additional fiber naturally found in your jam.

Summer is more relaxed and is the perfect time to be creative. Change things up a bit to a taste that suits you and your guests. Try different citrus fruits or berries, herbal teas, and every jam you own! You may, of course, add alcohol, but these summer beverages are primarily designed to quench one's thirst.

Non-alcoholic drinks are more refreshing and are best to keep you hydrated and healthy. Water is great, but you also need to make sure you are replacing lost salt, sugar, potassium and other nutrients for your body to function properly.

MARMALADE COCKTAILS PAST TO PRESENT

Marmalade cocktails are both classic and chic. Here are some delicious, quintessential recipes from the 1930's, 40's, 50's and today. Now it's your turn to try them out for yourself with one of LunaGrown's special marmalades.

One such durable innovation from the past, it's worth noting, is the use of marmalade in cocktails. When America succumbed to Prohibition, London became the capital of fancy drinks, many of which incorporated indigenous ingredients. "The cocktail, exiled to England by the Volstead Act, here shows some new and startling forms,"

The American Mercury reported at the time. "There are formulae for cocktails made of raspberries, sloe gin, bitter almonds, grape jelly, and even marmalade." *Ref: Wall Street Journal, July 2008*

The general definition for marmalade is a sweet jelly in which pieces of fruit and rind are suspended. The key is the rind, whose bitterness delightfully balances the sweetness of the jelly.

Most marmalades have a citrus base, either orange, lime, lemon, grapefruit, or kumquat. To this general base, many other fruits can be added to awaken the palate. Marmalade is traditionally used as a sweet spread variety of breads, but inventive chefs have taught us that citrus marmalades can also serve as an ingredient in desserts as well as sweet and savory sauces for meat, poultry, and vegetables, And lastly, these classic, vintage marmalade-made cocktails.

MARMALADE COCKTAILS

This is a delicious Gin based cocktail usually served as a luncheon aperitif found in the Savoy Cocktail Book, this recipe dates back to the 1930's.

Place the following mixture in the shaker:

- 2 tbsp marmalade.
- The Juice of 1 big or 2 small Lemons.
- 4 Glasses Gin

Shake carefully and pour out, squeezing a piece of orange rind into each glass.

OMAR BRADLEY

The G.I.'s favorite general, Omar Bradley (WWII), liked Old-Fashioneds, but who has fresh orange slices for muddling in the field? The story is told that General Omar Bradley, while campaigning through the deserts of North Africa, wanted to have an Old Fashioned, but didn't have citrus available. He substituted orange marmalade as an alternative to citrus.

- 2 oz bourbon or rye whiskey
- 1 tsp (heaping or not, to taste) orange marmalade
- 1 squeeze fresh lemon juice
- 1 dash Angostura bitters

Shake well with ice and strain into an Old-Fashioned glass with fresh ice. Garnish with a cherry.

Add a spoonful of Jam or Marmalade to your favorite Martini recipe and you'll be charmingly surprised. Add depth, richness and an elegant air. A chipotle jelly Martini will wow your friends for years to come!

KINLOCH PLANTATION SPECIAL

This recipe, for a whiskey punch of sorts with marmalade and nutmeg, appears in Charleston Receipts, the oldest junior league cookbook, in print from 1950.

- 2 oz bourbon whiskey
- (Charleston Receipts lists amount as a "Generous portion of whiskey")
- 1 heaping ½ tsp marmalade
- 2 pinches nutmeg
- splash of filtered water

Add marmalade and water to glass with a pinch of nutmeg. Stir into paste. Add whiskey and cracked ice, and stir. Top with another pinch of nutmeg. The original recipe suggests shaking but does not specify whether you should strain it or not. The marmalade will settle, so serve with a spoon or stirrer.

MARMALADE MARTINI

This recipe was created by a group of LunaGrown Marmalade fans. Originally created with Lemon Lavender Marmalade, has grown to include Blood Orange and Lime Marmalades as well.

- 3 oz Vodka or Gin
- 2 tbsp marmalade
- 2 dashes dry vermouth

Combine liquid ingredients in a cocktail shaker filled with ice; shake well. Pour liquid over mulled marmalade, Enjoy!

RUSSIAN MARTINI

No date could be found for this recipe, so your guess is as good as mine. Either way it's a delicious way to enjoy Russian Vodka!

- 2 oz Russian Vodka
- 1 tsp Orange Marmalade
- 4 Raspberries
- ½ oz Lemon Juice
- ¾ oz Simple Syrup

Shake well and strain into chilled martini glass. Garnish with an orange peel.

HOLIDAY COCKTAILS
WITH LUNAGROWN JAM

Warm your holidays with these deliciously creative cocktails utilizing jam. Whether it be a cold snowy afternoon or a cool winter's day at the beach, these cocktail recipes will add a little joy to your jingle bell hop. Do something extra special with your jam this holiday season!

RAZZLEBERRY JAM COCKTAIL

2½ oz. cognac
2½ oz. apple juice
½ oz. Agave Nectar
2 tbsp LunaGrown Razzleberry jam
3 blueberries and 2 raspberries (garnish)

Combine all ingredients in a cocktail shaker and shake well. Strain into a wine goblet filled with ice and garnish with an orange wedge and fresh raspberries.

This combination is also amazing warm!

PINK MANGO CHAMPAGNE

½ cup pomegranate juice
½ cup LunaGrown Mango jam
1 bottle champagne or sparkling cider, chilled
Fresh Strawberries for garnish

Combine Pomegranate juice and LunaGrown Mango Jam in a small sauce pan and heat, stir to combine creating a syrup. When combined remove from heat and allow to cool. Refrigerate until ready for use. Pour two to three teaspoons of the syrup into champagne flutes and top with champagne. Garnish with a fresh strawberry.

APPLE GINGERED BOURBON

3 oz apple cider
1½ ounces bourbon
2 oz ginger beer
1 tbsp LunaGrown Apple jam

Place a tablespoon of room temperature Jam in a heat proof glass mug. Combine cider, bourbon, and ginger beer. Warm in a small sauce pan (do not boil). Pour over jam and top with grated nutmeg. Garnish with apple or orange slices and cinnamon sticks.

This should warm up any cool day!

HOT CHOCOLATE RASPBERRY

1½ oz Chambord
1 oz. white crème de cacao
8 oz. hot chocolate
whipped cream
1 tbsp LunaGrown Raspberry jam

In a heat proof glass mug combine Chambord, crème de cacao, and hot chocolate. Top with whipped cream and a teaspoon of LunaGrown Raspberry Jam. Garnish with a peppermint stick or a sprig of fresh mint. With this beverage the jam will ease to the bottom and slowly release its fine fresh flavor.

Nothing is nicer than some sweet warm chocolate and berries during the holiday season!!!

SOME HELPFUL TIPS

HOW TO MAKE BUTTERMILK

- Milk (just under one cup)
- 1 tbsp white vinegar or lemon juice (lemon juice is preferred)
- Add the lemon juice to the one cup of milk and mix, allow to sit for five minutes and use as directed.

IMPORTANCE OF ROOM TEMPERATURE EGGS

- Ensures proper rise in baked goods as well as griddle cakes (pancakes, waffles, crepes).
- Creates a smoother more palatable texture in the finished product.

PROPERLY SERVING JAM

- Jam should be served (with meals) at room temperature or slightly warmed. This increases the intensity of the flavors and allows for an easier spread on warm items.

FAVORITE BUTTERMILK BISCUITS

Food history is amazing. Also it expands our appreciation for the food and the recipe itself. The earliest sweet biscuit to date would be what we know as "Gingerbread" created by the Persian Empire, and introduced in France around 995.

American biscuits are usually browned on the outer edges and softer in the center. Historically served with an evening meal, or with breakfast with molasses or fruit preserves.

Long ago when armies and explorers traveled by sea, in order to eat they would have to bring on their journey a chef and cattle so that the meals were fresh as there was no refrigeration then. This was expensive and took up a vast amount of room. It also shortened the voyage as food supplies had to be replenished. This led many to adopt the style of hunter-foraging.

The introduction of baking cereals and flour provided a more reliable and nutritious food source. From the early Egyptians through the Roman Empire we find recipes for baked biscuits and flat breads.

These items were usually packed for sea voyages and were created extra hard as moisture is abundant at sea and, as we know, moist bread gathers mold quicker. Biscuits were often baked four times and could last for years if properly stored.

Biscuits were usually served with brine, coffee, or another liquid warmed in a skillet. Hence biscuits and gravy. During the Spanish Armada the royal navy's daily ration per sailor were one pound of biscuits and one gallon of beer. This remained the staple ration for military voyages until the introduction of canned goods in 1847.

BUTTERMILK BISCUITS

INGREDIENTS

- 2 cups flour
- 3 tsp sugar
- 1 tbsp baking powder
- 1 tsp salt
- ½ tsp soda
- 6 Tbsp butter (well chilled)
- 1 cup buttermilk

INSTRUCTIONS

1. Combine all dry ingredients and mix well
2. Cut butter into chunks and slice into your dry mixture creating a flake like mixture
3. Add 1 cup of buttermilk *
4. Mix to create a sticky dough and layout on a floured surface
5. Hand pat the dough to about ½ inch thick and fold it in on itself. Remember to lightly flour as you do so. Repeat this set at least four times. Leaving the final dough thickness at around ¾ inch.
6. Cut dough with a circular object and place next to each other on a baking sheet
7. Bake in pre-heated 350° oven for 15-20 minutes or until tops are lightly golden
8. *Buttermilk can be created by combining ¾ cup of whole milk and ¼ cup of lemon juice or white vinegar. allow this to sit for 5 minutes without stirring.

BLUEBERRY CHEDDAR BISCUITS

Blueberry Cheddar biscuits are a perfect match with any jam or marmalade, but are especially delicious paired with Lemon Lavender Marmalade. You can't go wrong with fresh blueberries and your favorite sharp cheddar cheese. Adding that sweet note of Lemon Lavender Marmalade brings all the flavors together with just the right balance.

These Blueberry Cheddar Biscuits are so easy to create you'll be wishing blueberry season came faster! They are wonderful for breakfast, or even with afternoon tea or evening cocktails. Biscuits also make a thoughtful gift for a friend who might be feeling a bit blue. Be the envy of your social club with these delicious treats.

.

BLUEBERRY CHEDDAR BISCUITS

INGREDIENTS

- 2 cups of flour
- ⅔ cup of sugar
- ¼ tsp baking soda
- 1 tsp salt (do not omit)
- 1 tbsp baking powder
- 6 tbsp butter diced
- 1 cup buttermilk
- ½ tsp vanilla
- ¼ cinnamon
- *Add these ingredients and mix into a wet dough
- 1 cup (or so) fresh blueberries
- ½ cup freshly shredded sharp cheddar cheese

INSTRUCTIONS

1. Combine dry ingredients and mix well. Add diced butter and combine until the consistency of flakes or small peas
2. Now add your buttermilk, vanilla and cinnamon and mix well to get a sticky dough.
3. Using a rubber spatula or wooden spoon mix the berries and cheese into your dough. It will be sticky. You may add a tablespoon of flour so that you may form a ball with the dough.
4. Place dough on cutting board and with your hands pat the dough to around an inch thick.
5. Cut into round biscuits and place in greased pan or cast iron skillet and bake at 375° for 20-30 minutes or until the top is lightly browned.
6. Allow to cool for 5 minutes before serving with whipped butter and some LunaGrown Lemon Marmalade!

Baking is a combination of science and art. Recipes are combinations that treat our palate. Artfully done they bring us joyful memories for a lifetime.

BUTTERY VANILLA SCONES

There is an art to everything worth enjoying. This includes scones. It is important to take your time and enjoy the process – these are scones of distinction, not simple bowls of cereal. Here are a few tips from a master scone baker which we'll happily share with you.

The most important place to start is by purchasing high quality ingredients. A final product is the sum of all of its parts, so high quality flour, sugar, and butter are important.

While short cuts may work in many recipes they are best avoided when making scones. The time and care taken will show in the end result.

The best butter for baking is one with a higher fat content. Butter with added water will make an inferior biscuit or scone. Compare labels for the highest fat content.

Another important bit of advice is to start with icy cold butter and cut it into fine cubes or small pea size chunks, then put it in the freezer while you measure out everything else. It is important to work with the butter as cold as possible as you do not want the butter and the flour to cream together during the mixing process. The butter chunks will melt during baking, leaving those beautiful holes where the flavor collects.

Finally, the folding of your dough is especially important for scones. You must not simply roll it out and cut circles. By gently but quickly folding and re-folding the dough, you are creating those wonderful flaky buttery layers in the scones that your jam and cream will search out.

These simple scones are wonderful anytime of day and with most meals. Enjoy them, scones are better when shared with friends!

BUTTERY VANILLA SCONES

SCONES

- 1 cup cake flour (not self rising flour. This is important!)
- 2 cups all purpose flour
- ½ cup granulated white sugar
- 2 tsp baking powder
- ½ tsp baking soda
- ¼ tsp salt
- 1½ sticks unsalted, cold butter
- 1¼ cup buttermilk
- 1 tbsp vanilla

CREAM TOPPING

- 2 cups heavy whipping cream
- 1 tsp vanilla
- 1 tbsp sugar or honey
- pinch of salt

As you become more comfortable creating scones you might substitute vanilla for herbs such as basil or fresh mint. Working on the amount of buttermilk to allow for cheese or dried fruits might also be an option.

INSTRUCTIONS

1. Cut butter into small pieces, place in bowl and put in freezer to keep very cold.
2. Preheat oven to 375 degrees F (190 degrees C) and place rack in middle of oven. Line a baking sheet with parchment paper.
3. In a large bowl, whisk together the flour, sugar, baking powder, baking soda, and salt. Blend very cold butter into the flour mixture with a pastry blender or two knives. You want the mixture to look like coarse crumbs. Add the buttermilk and vanilla then stir just until the dough comes together (add more buttermilk if necessary).
4. place dough onto a lightly floured work surface; roll out into a rectangle. With a short side facing you, fold rectangle into thirds, as you would a letter. Rotate dough. Repeat rolling out, folding, and rotating dough 2 more times. With floured hands, pat out dough to a 1¼-inch thickness, and cut out as many rounds as possible with a floured 2¼-inch round biscuit cutter. Place scones on baking sheet.
5. Then, using your thumb, make an indentation in the middle of each scone, pressing down almost to the bottom of the scone. Try not to squash the outside edges of the scone. Fill each indentation with a scant tablespoon of LunaGrown jam.
6. Bake for about 20 minutes or until golden brown and a toothpick inserted in the middle of a scone comes out clean. Remove from oven and transfer to a wire rack to cool.

CREAM TOPPING

1. Either by hand or using a mixer whip heavy cream to a semi thick consistency
2. Add vanilla, salt and sweetener. Continue to whip the cream until desired consistency.
3. Serve atop warm scones.
4. *Note: If you over-whip the cream it will begin to become butter, at this point you might as well continue and serve your scones with sweet butter rather than whipped cream!

JAM FILLED BREAKFAST CRÊPES

This recipe may be used for breakfast, dessert or dinner crepes and filled with a myriad of items from jam and fruits to shrimp and chicken, cheese and vegetables.

While crepes are generally associated with France they are enjoyed world wide. Crepes can be found from France to Belgium, Quebec, Europe, Africa, South America and the United States.

A crêperie could be a takeaway food stand often found at the seaside or harbor. Crêperie may also be a sit down café or a restaurant where variations on the classic are served.

This recipe is a variation on a classic from 1958. The most popular crepe is served with warmed strawberry jam and whipped cream, the inclusion of fresh fruit, melted chocolate, and various warmed liquors help to endear this dish in our culture.

CRÊPES A LA LUNAGROWN

INGREDIENTS

- 1 cup plus 2 tablespoons whole milk
- 2 large eggs
- 1 cup all-purpose flour
- 2 tbsp granulated sugar
- 3 tbsp plus 1 tsp unsalted butter, melted and cooled slightly
- ¼ tsp salt
- 1 jar LunaGrown Jam
- 1 tbsp brandy
- Confectioners sugar

INSTRUCTIONS

1. Blend milk, eggs, flour, granulated sugar, 2 tablespoons butter, and salt in a blender, scraping down side once or twice, until batter is smooth, about 1 minute.
2. Let batter stand at room temperature 1 hour (this prevents tough crêpes).
3. Stir together jam and brandy in a small bowl.
4. Preheat oven to 250° F.
5. Add ½ teaspoon butter to skillet and brush to coat bottom.
6. Heat over moderate heat until hot, about 30 seconds, then pour ¼ cup batter into skillet, tilting to coat bottom evenly.
7. Cook until underside is pale golden, 1 ½ to 2 minutes, then jerk skillet to loosen crepe and flip crepe with a spatula.
8. Cook until underside is pale golden, 30 seconds to 1 minute.
9. Transfer crepe with spatula to a work surface, turning over so that side cooked first is face down.
10. Spread 1 tablespoon jam all over crepe and roll up jelly-roll style.
11. Transfer to a heatproof platter and keep warm in oven.
12. Make 7 more crêpes in same manner, transferring to oven. Arrange rolled crêpes side by side.

- Enjoy a variation of Crêpe Suzette by employing orange or lemon marmalade with Grand Marnier some sweet butter and powdered sugar.

The first time someone has crepes, no matter their age, will create a memory they'll carry with them their whole life. The experience is to be relished. Make sure it is special for everyone to live and relive.

BELGIAN WAFFLES WITH LUNAGROWN JAM AND FRESH FRUIT

Traditional Belgian waffles are created with a yeast batter which sits overnight and is cooked the next morning. These are created with baking soda to shorten the waiting time. It is still suggested you allow the batter to sit at least 30 minutes to allow the leavening agents to do their job.

When it comes to flavor combinations and Belgian waffles think carnival. Go wild! Pictured above: Belgian waffles with berry jam, dark chocolate, pineapple, bananas, watermelon, maple syrup, fresh whipped cream and a sprinkle of powdered sugar.

Belgian waffles are a treat and should be enjoyed for the experience they offer. These waffles also make a surprising addition to ice cream as a serving base or as a sandwich.

Belgian waffles are wonderful served with raspberry jam, chocolate sauce, fresh whipped cream and a brandy syrup or perhaps with a side of melon and shrimp or oysters. The combinations are endless and fresh Belgian waffles beg for indulgence!

Belgian Waffles are a reminder of late brunch at the seaside. They should be light, full of flavor and have an air of carefree decadence.

BELGIAN WAFFLES

INGREDIENTS

Belgian Waffles make a tasteful breakfast or brunch dish. However, they are also divine with ice cream as a sandwich and as a bread, for a variation of the Monte Christo Sandwich.

- 1 cup flour
- ¼ cup cornstarch
- ½ tsp baking powder
- ¼ tsp baking soda
- ½ tsp salt
- 1 cup buttermilk (do not substitute)
- ⅓ cup melted butter
- 1 egg, room temperature and separated
- ⅓ cup sugar
- 1½ tsp vanilla

INSTRUCTIONS

1. In a bowl beat the egg white until stiff peaks form. Set aside.
2. In a medium bowl, combine the flour, cornstarch, baking powder, baking soda, and salt; mix well.
3. Add the milk, butter, egg yolk, sugar and vanilla and mix just until combined. Do not over mix as you do not want air in this. Some lumps are OK.
4. Gently fold in the egg whites until combined. Do not deflate the egg whites. This is what will give your waffles that light texture.
5. Let the batter sit for 30 minutes.
6. Heat a waffle iron. and follow the manufacturers directions to cook the waffles.
7. Serve immediately or hold in a warm oven, directly on the rack. Avoid stacking while keeping warm.
8. To freeze, allow to cool completely and wrap individually in plastic wrap.
9. To reheat just place frozen in the toaster.

BUTTERMILK PANCAKES WITH JAM

Pancakes for breakfast, lunch or dinner. Depending of course on what you serve them with.

Traditionally pancakes are served as part of breakfast with eggs and sausage. However, pancakes can easily be utilized as a bread for lunch or a replacement for dinner biscuits. Adding jam extends your options one step farther.

Jam on breakfast pancakes with some fresh fruit and whipped cream is a great way to begin the morning. Using a pancake as a wrap for a sweet luncheon bread with raspberry jam, roast beef, kale and goat cheese is brilliant. An evening meal with roast pork a small stack, brandy pork gravy, fig jam and sautéed vegetables is heavenly on an Autumn evening.

This recipe makes quite a stack of pancakes. Layer jam between the pancakes, maybe add some syrup, some pecans or walnuts, a bit of whipped cream, perhaps some cream cheese and you'll have a beautiful dessert pancake.

HOMEMADE PANCAKES

INGREDIENTS

- 2 cups all-purpose flour
- ¼ cup granulated sugar
- 2½ tsp. baking powder
- ½ tsp. baking soda
- ½ tsp. salt
- 2 cups buttermilk
- 2 large eggs

MAKING BUTTERMILK:

- Milk (just under one cup)
- 1 Tablespoon white vinegar or lemon juice (lemon juice is preferred)
- Add the lemon juice to the one cup of milk and mix, allow to sit for five minutes and use as directed.

INSTRUCTIONS

1. Thoroughly mix the dry ingredients (and save this recipe so you never have to pay for pancake mix again). I prefer to mix the wet ingredients together and then combine the wet and dry. Do not over-mix this as your pancakes will not rise correctly.
2. Prepare a stick of butter by cutting it into pats to put on the pancakes as they are transferred from the skillet to a plate.
3. On a greased, heated skilled pour about a three inch circle of batter (it will spread out a bit) once bubbles form on the top, flip the cake and cook a bit longer. Remove to a dish on the side and butter while it's hot.

Pancakes are also known as griddlecakes, flapjacks or hotcakes and are among the food items created world wide. The first commercial pancake mix was Aunt Jemima Pancake Flour in 1889.

GRANOLA, JAM AND YOGURT START YOUR DAY OFF BRIGHT!

Many people frequently skip their breakfast, but were you aware that a good breakfast is probably the most crucial meal of your entire day? Filling up with healthy goodness to start helps to pump up your metabolism and will likely keep you sharp all day. A great start with granola, jam and yogurt will keep you going and keep your mind alert!

Many people also choose a handy sugar loaded snack to help get them through the day rather than a well balanced one. We suggest trying the alternatives herein to help give you that needed boost of energy and nutrition rather than the coffee and chocolate bar.

Granola contains oats, which are a whole grain. The Harvard School of Public Health published a study in 2017 that confirmed the regular consumption of whole grains can help reduce risk factors for heart disease and diabetes.

Whole grains are an important source of fiber which can regulate your digestive system. Granola often also includes nutrient-rich dried fruit and nuts.

Yogurt is often found on healthy food lists and for good reason. Yogurt is highly nutritious and is an excellent source of protein, calcium and potassium.

Yogurt provides numerous vitamins and minerals and is relatively low in calories.

The current Dietary Guidelines for Americans recommend that individuals ages nine and older consume three servings of milk, cheese or yogurt each day; children 4-8 years should consume 2-1/2 servings. One serving of yogurt is one eight-ounce cup or container.

Granola is made of rolled oats, nuts, honey or other sweeteners such as brown sugar, and sometimes puffed rice, that is usually baked until it is crisp, toasted and golden brown .

JAM, GRANOLA & YOGURT PARFAIT

- 4 tbsp of your favorite LunaGrown Jam
- 6 oz. Greek yogurt
- ¾ Cup Granola

Spoon 2 Tbsp. preserves into the bottom of a 12 oz. jar or cereal bowl.
Sprinkle half the granola over preserves and top with yogurt.
Spoon remaining 2 Tbsp. preserves over yogurt and top with remaining granola to serve.

Plain yogurt becomes memorable with the addition of berry jam and a sprinkle of granola. During the warmer months choose, or make, frozen yogurt to invigorate your day.

Using rolled oats you may create your own granola specific to your liking. Make the beginning of your day the best that it can be.

JAM AND GRANOLA DESSERT PARFAIT

9 oz (1 jar) LunaGrown Jam
2 cup low-fat plain yogurt
2 oz fat free cream cheese
1 tbsp honey
4 tsp ground cinnamon
1 cup granola

Combine yogurt, cream cheese, honey, and cinnamon in a small bowl; beat with an electric mixer on medium speed till combined.

Chill for 1/2 hour. To assemble, layer LunaGrown Jam, yogurt-cheese mixture, and your favorite granola as desired in individual dishes. Serve immediately.

Many people have asked which is the best jam and granola to use in their parfait, my suggestion is to start with your favorite jam paired with a high quality granola and a plain yogurt or kefir. You can experiment from there with your mixtures. The flavor decisions are up to you and your palate.

BREADS

SWEET NORTHERN CORNBREAD

One article suggests that cornbread was well known to the indigenous peoples of America long before the English settlers. However its form would have been closer to what we now know as a tortilla. The English settlers combined the corn meal with eggs and water. These were known as Jonny cakes. Jonny cakes were similar to today's pancake and utilized honey or molasses or maple as a sweet topping.

Domesticated corn was developed in Mexico and made its way into the South. Southern slaves are credited for creating the basis of what we now call cornbread. This was known as Kush or "Cush" (depending on the area) and was a cornbread stuffing. This consisted of salt meat grease to treat the pan, crumbled up cornmeal, a bit of water, and wild onions, herbs, and red peppers. The corn was a white corn.

By the 1930's the Kush or Cornbread stuffing had been tweaked as most recipes are and in the south included a bit of white flour and baking soda to help it rise. It still contained no sugar and was considered something served with dinner.

In the 1930's a company in Michigan started making baking mixes "So easy even a man can do it" Jiffy, was created as the first prepared baking mix in the United States by Mabel White Holmes. This brought a standard cornbread to the bulk of the country. Jiffy is still owned and operated by the same family and employees about 300 workers in Chelsea, Michigan.

Okay the sugar, the real honest to goodness reason for cornbread with and without sugar. Ask your farmer! Originally northern corn was a yellow corn variety, not very sweet (needed some sweetener). Southern corn was usually the white variety, which is a sweet corn. The southwestern corn was Blue corn, even milled almost too gritty for cornbread.

Farmers grew (and still do) what the land and location would offer the best and healthiest yields. The corn brought by the English died fast due to rust and blight. So healthy corn crops, grown in different regions and with different characteristics are why Southern cornbread has no sugar, and northern cornbread does. Sweet corn vs. Not so Sweet Corn.

Cranberry Jam or Orange Marmalade makes a nice addition to this Northern Cornbread as do most berry jams.

By adding an additional egg you can utilize this recipe to make corncakes, a variation on pancakes. These make an excellent side dish served with fresh tomato salsa, cilantro and Chipotle or Hot Pepper Jelly. They are tasteful served hot or cold.

When it comes to cornbread, the sweet northern variety seems to lend itself to a fruit jam, whereas the true southern variety seems better suited for a chipotle or hot pepper jelly.

SWEET NORTHERN CORNBREAD

INGREDIENTS

- 1 cup all purpose flour
- 1 cup yellow cornmeal (you can use white if need be)
- ½ cup sugar
- 1 tbsp brown sugar
- 1 tbsp baking powder
- 1 tsp salt
- 1 egg
- 1 cup buttermilk
- ⅓ cup melted butter
- ½ tsp vanilla

INSTRUCTIONS

1. Pre-heat oven to 375 degrees
2. Spray or lightly grease a 9 inch square glass pan
3. Combine all dry ingredients and mix well
4. Add egg, buttermilk, butter, and vanilla. mix well (do not over mix)
5. Pour into greased pan
6. Bake in preheated oven for 25 to 30 minutes or until a toothpick inserted into the center comes out clean

COCONUT BREAD

Making a marmalade glaze is easy and creates an impressive finish to any sweet bread. Simply warm your favorite marmalade in a glass measuring cup until liquid, slowly pour over your favorite bread allowing the marmalade to cool as you go, thus creating a beautiful glaze.

INGREDIENTS

- ½ cup butter, softened
- 1 cup sugar
- 2 eggs
- 1 tsp vanilla extract
- 2 cups all-purpose flour
- 2 tsp baking powder
- ½ tsp salt
- ¾ cup coconut milk (specifically!)
- 1¼ cups flaked coconut

INSTRUCTIONS

1. In a large bowl, cream butter and sugar until light and fluffy. *Add* eggs, one at a time, beating well after each addition. Beat in vanilla.
2. Combine the flour, baking powder and salt; gradually add to creamed mixture alternately with milk, beating well after each addition. Stir in coconut.
3. Pour into a greased 9-in.x 5-in. loaf pan. Bake at 350° for 1 hour or until a toothpick inserted near the center comes out clean.
4. Cool for 10 minutes before removing from pan to a wire rack to cool completely.
5. Serve with Lime Marmalade or top with a lime marmalade glaze and coconut flakes.

MOIST APPLE MUFFINS

There is nothing nicer than starting the day with a hearty apple muffin, warm and fragrant, fresh from the oven. You could enjoy one with afternoon tea or pack them into lunchboxes. If you love autumn spices and you love apples then these are the muffins for you! Serve these muffins with Cinnamon Raisin Jam, Spiced Fig Jam or Cranberry Jam.

Fresh Golden Delicious or Cortland apples are usually the sweetest and the best for baking, however you can certainly use end of season apples. Not to be confused with pie apples, Gala, Granny Smith or Winesap which have a tart flavor that sweetens during the cooking process.

These muffins are memorably moist and low in sugar, making them perfect for anytime of the day. You may choose to make a double batch and freeze some for a later time.

Making someone feel special has never been easier, and is always appreciated. Line a seasonal basket with an inexpensive tea towel and batch of muffins. Add a jar of jam, a favorite book and you have a perfect gift!

MOIST APPLE MUFFINS

INGREDIENTS

- 1¾ cup flour
- ½ cup sugar
- 2 tbsp baking powder
- 1 tsp baking soda
- 1 tsp cinnamon
- 1 tsp nutmeg
- 1 tsp vanilla
- 5 tbsp butter (melted)
- 1 egg
- 1 cup sour cream
- 2 cups peeled and diced apples

INSTRUCTIONS

1. Pre-heat oven to 400
2. Combine dry ingredients and mix well
3. Add all wet ingredients including apples and mix by hand making sure all ingredients are well blended but not over mixed (don't try to whip the batter)
4. Spoon into greased muffin tins, filling about ⅔
5. Bake at 400 for 10 minutes, lower temperature to 350 and continue to bake until the tops are browned and an inserted toothpick comes out clean.
6. Remove from oven and remove muffins from tins, set on cooling rack.
7. Enjoy

The best thing about apple muffins and jam is they make a thoughtful gift that could brighten a person's day. Everyone could use a brighter day now and again.

BLOOD ORANGE MARMALADE AND DATE NUT BREAD

There are three main types of blood oranges: Moro, Tarocco and Sanguinello. Blood oranges are generally available in the United States from December to April. Moros are the most common blood oranges in the USA. They are pleasingly sweet-tart flavored and some compare them to oranges with a hint of raspberry flavor.

Tarocco blood oranges are less popular, however they remain especially cherished in Italy and throughout Europe, for their delicate, sweet flavor. A Sanguinello blood orange often has a rose-tinted rind, yet its flesh is usually a lighter dappled mix of red and yellow.

Anthocyanin, the red pigment that provides the blood orange's distinctive coloration, is an antioxidant. Since the most brightly colored foods are also the ones packed with the most cancer-fighting antioxidants, blood oranges are a powerhouse of nutrition. They are also a great source of vitamin C, fiber and potassium.

Blood Orange marmalade is one of LunaGrown's most popular jams and is one of our personal favorites. We hope you take the time to try some this winter season. One way to enjoy Blood Orange marmalade is spread on a slice of date nut bread. This recipe was originally published in Good Housekeeping, and has been a favorite for many years. Enjoy with our Blood Orange marmalade or one of our other popular marmalades!

Blood Orange Marmalade is certainly a specialty item as blood oranges are not easy to find year round. The marmalade is a rare treat. A compliment to this beautiful Date Nut Bread.

Date Nut Bread

INGREDIENTS

- 1 container (10 ounces) pitted dates, finely chopped
- 6 tbsp margarine or butter, cut up
- 2 cups all-purpose flour
- ¾ cup sugar
- 1 tsp baking powder
- ½ tsp baking soda
- ½ tsp salt
- 1 large egg, lightly beaten
- 1 cup pecans, coarsely chopped

INSTRUCTIONS

1. In 2-quart saucepan, heat 1¼ cups water to boiling over high heat. Remove saucepan from heat; stir in dates and margarine or butter. Let stand until cool, about 30 minutes.
2. Preheat oven to 325 degrees F. Grease 9- by 5-inch loaf pan.
3. In large bowl, combine flour, sugar, baking powder, baking soda, and salt. With fork, stir egg into cooled date mixture; stir into flour mixture just until evenly moistened (do not overmix). Stir in pecans. Spoon batter into loaf pan and spread evenly.
4. Bake bread 1 hour 10 minutes or until toothpick inserted in center of loaf comes out clean. Cool bread in pan on wire rack 10 minutes. Remove from pan and cool completely on rack. Cut into slices to serve.

WARM JAM AND CINNAMON BUNS

These delightful cinnamon buns are a family favorite. Take time when creating this treat for your family. The process should make you feel that much closer to the ones you love.

Enjoy them plain or with just a bit of icing. However, you may find they are beyond compare when served with warm apple jam, orange marmalade, or colorful raspberry and strawberry jams.

These cinnamon buns are nothing like store bought. These are a hearty bun. They are thick and sweet not fried and oily. These cinnamon buns take time to create, so be prepared to wait. The more patience you have the better your cinnamon buns will turn out.

Cinnamon buns fill any kitchen with warm memories, kind thoughts of the past, and smiles for a bright future. These sweet buns make a wonderful gift, include your favorite jam and share some heartfelt smiles with old friends and new.

OLD FASHIONED CINNAMON BUNS

INGREDIENTS

- 6 cups of flour
- 2 tsp Himalayan salt
- 1½ tbsp instant yeast
- ¾ plus 1 tbsp sugar
- 1½ cups water
- ½ stick melted butter
- ½ cup cinnamon and sugar
- ¼ cup oil

Good yeast bread takes time and patience, but it's always well worth the wait! These Cinnamon Buns certainly are no exception. Take your time and enjoy the process, then enjoy it again with someone worth your time.

INSTRUCTIONS

1. Combine yeast and 1 tbsp sugar in a glass measuring cup. Add to this 1½ cups of water at 120 degrees. Mix with wooden spoon until dissolved. Set aside and allow yeast to activate. Volume in glass measuring cup should double.
2. In a mixing bowl add 4 cups of flour, 1 cup of sugar and the salt. Combine ingredients well.
3. Using your hands or a hook attachment for your mixer, slowly add liquid to your flour combination. add oil and 1 more cup of flour until a soft dough is formed that loosely holds it's shape.
4. Grease a glass bowl, place dough in bowl, cover and set aside in warm area. Allow dough to rise at least 4 hours.
5. When dough has risen remove from bowl and punch down. On a flat surface, using a rolling pin, roll dough out to approximately ¼ inch thick. brush with melted butter and sprinkle your cinnamon sugar mixture onto the dough. you may go as heavy or as light as you like.
6. Roll dough into a cylinder shape. seal end with additional melted butter and pinch together. cut rolls using string or clean dental floss around 1" think.
7. Place in greased glass baking dish with at least ½ - ¾ inches space between them. Cover and set in warm place again allow to rise about 2 hours.
8. Bake in preheated oven at 350 for 35 minutes. You may choose to brush melted butter over the tops 10 minutes prior to removing from oven.
9. Enjoy

DINNER

GREEN SALAD WITH JAM DRESSING

The most wonderful things about green salads are that there are no rules, and there are so many flavors and textures to choose from when creating one. There are three main types of lettuce for instance, head, leaf and cob. Within these types of lettuce there are a vast array of choices. Choose at least three when creating a good green salad base, and try to change at least one each time for added interest.

Tomatoes and onions also come in many varieties, colors, textures and flavors. Thankfully we are seeing a reintroduction of many heirloom tomatoes thanks to our local farmers and farm markets. Again exploring the options can give you the opportunity to use your salad plate as a canvas. How can anyone resist exploring the colors, let alone the flavors and textures?

One can never have too much fruit in their diet. It's healthy, it's tasty, it's unique unto itself. Fruit, both fresh and dried, in a green salad gives your palate an unexpected burst of flavor. That touch of unexpected sweetness balances the occasional bitterness of the greens. Berries are a nice addition as they don't brown like some fruits.

Cheeses, nuts, meats, and even croutons are all delicious and add layers of flavor to any salad. Whether you choose one or many, they each add another dimension to the experience in terms of flavor, appearance, and texture.

Finally, there is the dressing. A homemade dressing is just as easy as a store bought one. There are thousands of recipes to be found so one could go wild with exploration. Below is a standard go to dressing. You can change the jam flavor and spices to suit your desires but this is a nice standard favorite to serve with any combination of greens.

There are some amazing dressings for both salads and sandwiches you can create with jam. There are even some beautiful dipping sauces that can be used for dressings or spreads as well. Don't limit yourself, explore!

STRAWBERRY JAM VINAIGRETTE

INGREDIENTS

- ⅓ cup white wine vinegar (you might prefer a different type, but I find the white wine vinegar doesn't step on the other flavors as a balsamic vinegar does)
- 3-4 tbsp Strawberry Jam (again you might choose another flavor jam to suit your meal)
- ¼ tsp crushed red pepper flakes
- ⅛ tsp salt (optional)

INSTRUCTIONS

Thoroughly mix the above ingredients together and then add:

1. ½ cup of Flaxseed or Hemp oil (keep in mind that you want oil with only a small hint of flavor as to not overpower your other ingredients)
2. It is preferable to let this dressing sit before serving to allow the flavors to combine well. Store in a sealed container in the refrigerator after use.

ADDITIONAL COMBINATIONS FOR SALADS AND SANDWICHES

- Cranberry jam with Dijon mustard
- Mango jam with rice wine and nut butter
- Hot pepper jam with mayonnaise
- Blueberry jam and Balsamic Vinegar
- Apple jam with sour cream

DRESSINGS

JEZEBEL SAUCE

INGREDIENTS

- 1 Jar (9 oz) Apple Jam
- 1 Jar (9 oz) Pineapple Jam
- 2 tbsp Mustard
- 1 tbsp Prepared Horseradish *to taste
- 1 tsp Fresh cracked black pepper

INSTRUCTIONS

1. Place all ingredients in food processor and mix well.
2. Store overnight on the counter.
3. Second day, spoon into plastic containers. Keeps in refrigerator for up to two weeks.
4. Serve with crackers and cheese or with BBQ

SWEET AND SOUR PLUM SAUCE

INGREDIENTS

- 1 can crushed pineapple in syrup
- 1 c. sugar
- 1 c. water
- 1 c. vinegar
- 1 tbsp. soy sauce
- 2 tbsp. cornstarch
- 2 tbsp. cold water
- 1 (9 oz) jar plum jam or orange marmalade

INSTRUCTIONS

1. Heat pineapple with syrup, sugar, water, vinegar and soy sauce to boiling.
2. Mix cornstarch and 2 tablespoons cold water, stir into pineapple mixture.
3. Heat to boiling, stirring constantly. Cool to room temperature, stir in plum jam.
4. Cover and refrigerate.
5. Serve as a dipping sauce with meats, or vegetables.

ACORN SQUASH CARAMELIZED WITH GREEN TOMATO JAM

A thick slice of artisan grain bread, toasted, buttered, and slathered with Green Tomato jam is a favorite snack. It is also enjoyable paired with a tangy sharp cheese - the sharper the better!

Some might wrinkle their noses at the thought of enjoying green tomatoes. Tomatoes are a fruit, botanically speaking, and not unlike their cousin the apple, they are delicious when prepared correctly no matter red or green.

Green tomatoes offer the same amount of beta carotene as ripened ones. If you did not know, you would never recognize green tomatoes as being in the tomato family. They are firm and tart. Green tomatoes may be eaten pickled, fried, or made into jam.

The following advice is invaluable when approaching green tomato jam for the first time. "Think of Green Tomato Jam as a chutney and take it from there."

"I love it in grilled cheese with a nice sharp cheddar. It's great with smoked turkey on sourdough bread. You can bake it with Brie Cheese and serve it on crackers or mix with mayonnaise or sour cream as a dip."

Roasted acorn squash with Green Tomato Jam. Acorn Squash as well as others are in season during the fall and make a delicious and healthy side dish or even a main course. This is a hearty Autumn treat. Easy to prepare, beautiful to present and flavors abound! Dinner for two or dinner for twelve our Green Tomato Jam with Acorn Squash a guaranteed hit.

ROASTED ACORN SQUASH WITH GREEN TOMATO JAM.

INGREDIENTS

- 2 acorn squash (about 1½ pounds each), un-peeled, cut in half and scooped clean
- 1 cup diced carrots, turnips, scallions
- Coarse salt and ground pepper
- 1 jar Green Tomato Jam

INSTRUCTIONS

1. Preheat oven to 450 degrees.
2. On a large rimmed baking sheet, place squash open side up.
3. Sprinkle salt and pepper on the diced vegetables and place inside the open squash.
4. Add one to two tablespoons of Green Tomato Jam to the top of your vegetables, then roast until easily pierced with a paring knife, 35 to 45 minutes.

Lucky for most, green tomato jam and acorn squash come into season about the same time every year. A wonderful combination to look forward to.

PINEAPPLE BBQ SAUCE

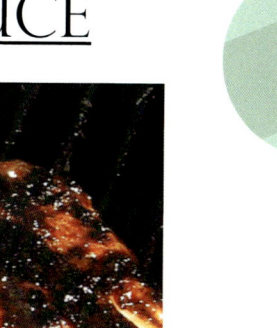

The word 'Barbecue' might come from the Taino Indian word 'barbacoa' meaning meat-smoking apparatus. 'Barbecue' could have also originated from the French word "Barbe a queue" which means "whiskers-to-tail." No one is sure of the correct origins of the word, but one thing is certain. Barbecue and grilling are two very different cooking processes.

True barbecue is an all-day event where meat is very slowly cooked over coals rendered down from flavorful smoking woods. By slowly cooking the meat over wood, it becomes infused with the smoke and the natural wood flavors. Different woods provide a different flavor.

The art of BBQ is traced back to the 1800's during western cattle drives. The cowboys often ate meats that were stringy and tough, such as rabbit or wild boar, which needed a long period of slow cooking to tenderize.

The likely hood of having fresh meat as we know it today was a rarity indeed as there was no way to keep it fresh and as it spoiled would attract scavengers.

What's the difference between BBQ and Grilling? BBQ is slow cooking with indirect heat and grilling is fairly quick cooking with a direct heat source. Sauces and glazed may be used for both applications.

The art of BBQ pork is a tradition deeply rooted in the south. Pork was a staple in most homes and every part of the animal utilized. However, pork was a tough meat that needed a slow cooking process. As BBQ pork became well known and considered an art, southerners began raising pigs with more fat on them to enhance the tenderness of the meat.

During the American Civil War and the consequential migration of the military, Southern BBQ was introduced to hungry Northern soldiers. After the war ended, the technique traveled further into the northern regions and expanded to other types of meats and poultry.

Today's culture brings us many styles of BBQ. The classic, dry- rubbed and marinated slow-smoked BBQ, is a favorite for many. The more common backyard cookout is sometimes preferred due to its ease of preparation and clean up. No matter how you BBQ, nothing beats a great sauce to highlight your cooking talents.

PINEAPPLE JAM BBQ SAUCE

INGREDIENTS

- 2 cups ketchup
- ⅓ cup apple vinegar
- ⅓ cup brown sugar
- 2 tbsp honey
- 2 tbsp Worcestershire sauce
- 3 tbsp spicy mustard
- 3 tbsp LunaGrown Pineapple Jam
- 1 tbsp onion powder
- 1 tbsp garlic powder
- ½ tsp cayenne pepper
- ½ tsp cinnamon

INSTRUCTIONS

1. Combine the above ingredients and mix well. Heat in a sauce pot on medium heat and bring to a boil stirring occasionally. Lower temperature and simmer for 15-20 minutes stirring to avoid scalding. Allow to cool.
2. This sauce is always better if you make it a day ahead of time. Store the sauce in the refrigerator for up to a month. If you are looking for a smokey flavored BBQ sauce you may add ½ tsp of liquid smoke per cup of sauce.

WE'RE LOVING LIME MARMALADE

A marmalade contains the skin or the rind of the fruit it was made from, this allows the marmalade to offer sweetness balanced with a bitter hint. A beautiful combination.

Many ask the question, "What do you do with Lime Marmalade" fairly often. To some this might seem silly, but if you are not familiar with Lime Marmalade, it's a fair question. Strawberry jam and grape jelly are more readily available and easily recognized, but Lime Marmalade, like most marmalades, is a rare treat in the United States. So, what to do with it when you are lucky enough to discover some?

- Lime marmalade makes a wonderful glaze for chicken and fish. Just heat a spoonful or two in a small sauce pan, add a dash of water or tequila to thin, and stir until well-combined. Cook your chicken or fish as desired, then glaze with your lime marmalade. When the glaze is bubbly turn chicken or fish over and glaze the opposite side. Delicious!
- Lime marmalade is a classic addition to your gin or vodka martini.
- Add some texture to a tomato, mango salad with lime marmalade and some Mexican spices. Go from salad to topping for burritos or taquitos.

- As we often suggest, Lime Marmalade makes a wonderful base for a dipping sauce. Using about 1/2 a jar, add cilantro and horseradish to taste. I prefer heavy on the cilantro! Again, you might add a touch of tequila if it suits you. This dipping sauce is excellent with chicken skewers or prepared taquitos.
- Raisin walnut bread from the farmers market with cream cheese and Lime marmalade is an uplifting way to begin your morning.
- Lime Marmalade makes a wonderful spicy pork roast glaze with a bit of tequila, some cilantro, and some thinly sliced jalapeno peppers.
- Create a beautiful salad dressing with Lime Marmalade, a nice virgin olive or black walnut oil, and an Italian wine vinegar. This dressing, some local goat cheese and fresh greens will leave you wanting for nothing more.
- Lime Marmalade with a Fino Sherry as a glaze for veal shoulder chops is outstanding.
- Try some Welsh pancakes. These are crepes spread with Marmalade and rolled up. Enjoy!

SWEET AND SOUR MEATBALLS

Sweet and sour meatballs or use Lil-Smokies. Great for football season, family picnics, pot luck, parties and more!

Substitute one jar of Grape Jelly for a jar of Chipotle Pepper Jelly for some unexpected Smokey warmth, a guaranteed favorite on game day.

Sweet and Sour Meatballs (or Cocktail Sausages)

- 1 12 oz jar Chili Sauce
- 2 9 oz jar LunaGrown Grape Jelly
- 2lb frozen meatballs or 2-3 packages cocktail sausages
- Pinch cayenne pepper

- *note that you could use one 9 oz jar of jelly instead. I like the sweetness of two jars, but you could make it less sweet with the one jar if you prefer.

- Combine jelly and chili sauce in a crock pot an stir until smooth. Heat the mixture if needed to combine. Add meatballs or cocktail sausages and set temperature to low. Cook for 2-5 hours on low. Serve with toothpicks.

- If you double the recipe, combine the grape jelly with the chili sauce in a large pot on the stove; add in the meatballs and simmer for about 45 minutes uncovered or until the sauce has thickened.

JAM GLAZE, SAUTÉ' AND GRAVY

Adding a special touch of flavor to your meals is an often overlooked use of jams and jellies. Here the jam maker shares the basics used in to enhance dishes with glazes, sautés, and gravies made with Jam.

GLAZES

When it comes to glazing meats or baked goods it is important to decide what your outcome should be. Are you hoping for a thick solid glaze like you would see on a fresh fruit tart or a thinner glaze often found on meats that just lightly enhances the dish.

For a thicker glaze finish, often seen on desserts you want to make sure that your end product is cooled, be that a cake or meats or anything else you are glazing. Remove from the jar the amount of jam you will need, keeping in mind the thickness of your glaze. You may warm the jam up in a sauce pan stirring constantly until it becomes liquid, Be very careful not to let the jam boil or it will not firm up again.

Pour your heated jam or brush it onto your creation and allow to cool completely.

For a thinner glaze often seen on poultry and pork you may follow the above steps adding spices if you desire, Rosemary makes a nice touch, and then brush onto the warm meat, drawing it up from the base as it cools.

For pastry it is best to use a jelly for glazing, for meats it is best to use a jam. One offers a translucent covering, while the other is more opaque with bits of fruit and spices.

SAUTÉ

Sautéed vegetables and beef medallions are a favorite, combined with a nice traditional jam, the flavor just pushes the envelope to the edge. When utilizing jam in this process you would sauté your vegetables or meat as usual with your oil or butter, lightly dressed with spices and just prior to the finish add a tablespoon or two of your favorite jam. The jam as it warms will temporarily liquefy and then become thicker again as it cools with your dish. The consistency will be that of a light gravy. As it cools, the flavors that have become part of your meat and vegetables will give you additional depth. Again remember not to allow this to reach a boil as it negatively affects the structure of the jam.

GRAVIES

This is a very simple trick learned in the restaurant business long ago. On occasion dishes such as grilled chicken breast with a pineapple rum sauce, or a 16 oz rib eye with a cranberry pecan sauce would be served. They sound fancy don't they. The trick is a heated gravy base, with alcohol and jam or nuts added, brought to a boil point. Quickly whisked and poured over the main dish. The combinations are endless.

Another amazing use of jam, adding a touch of sweetness to a memorable meal.

- Heat gravy in small skillet, bring to a boil
- Add 2 tbsp of jam to taste whisk rapidly
- Remove from heat
- Add alcohol of your choice whisk rapidly
- Pour over dish and serve

A table spoon of jam or marmalade added to a standard meat gravy adds depth and can be the highlight of your meal.

HOLIDAY DINNER WITH LUNAGROWN

LunaGrown is pleased to share with you some of our favorite holiday recipes. We begin with a wonderful holiday cocktail and goat cheese appetizer. Next our Pineapple Glazed Ham served with sautéed carrots and parsnips in a nice apricot sauce, choose a dessert that is memorable and enjoy

Notable flavors and great company make holiday meals memorable. Jam and marmalade can help by adding a touch of the extravagant.

ABERDEEN FLIP

The Aberdeen Flip is a wonderfully rich cocktail with hints of spice and fruit that will cheer any holiday gathering. For this cocktail you will need:

- 2 oz Chivas 18
- 1 oz sherry
- 1 egg
- ¼ oz spiced syrup
- dash chocolate bitters
- tsp blackberry jam
- grated nutmeg

To Prepare:

1. Dry shake all ingredients hard, add ice, shake hard again & strain into sherry glass.
2. Dust with grated nutmeg.

GOAT CHEESE AND RASPBERRY JAM

Tart raspberry jam and subtle, creamy goat cheese layered on a water cracker, garnished with a mint leaf.

You will need the following items:

- 1 cup Raspberry jam
- 1 block good quality goat cheese
- 1 package water crackers
- 20 mint leaves

To prepare:

1. Chill goat cheese until quite firm. Slice into discs 1/4 inch thick.
2. Place a disc of goat cheese on a water cracker and top with a teaspoon of raspberry jam. Garnish with a mint leaf. Repeat with remaining ingredients.

PINEAPPLE GLAZED HAM

A wonderfully moist and flavorful ham.

You will need the following items:

- 8 lb bone-in ham
- 8 cups pineapple juice
- 1 cup brown sugar
- 1 cup water
- 1 cup Pineapple jam

Follow these directions to prepare:

1. In a bowl, dissolve brown sugar in water. Pour in a large stockpot together with the ham and pineapple juice. Make sure ham is fully submerged in juice, add more juice or water if needed.
2. Bring to a boil, lower heat and cook for 1 hour. Set aside to cool.
3. Transfer ham in a roasting pan, score skin and fat into diamond shapes. Spread pineapple jam all around the ham.
4. Bake ham uncovered at pre-heated 400°F oven for 40 minutes or until well browned, basting once with juice from bottom of pan.
5. Let ham stand covered for 15 minutes before carving. Enjoy!!!

SAUTÉED CARROTS AND PARSNIPS WITH APRICOT JAM

The natural sugars in the vegetables work beautifully with the apricot jam to give it the perfect sticky and flavorful finish.

You will need the following:

- 1 lb small carrots, peeled and tops trimmed
- 1 lb small parsnips, peeled and halved (if larger than the carrots)
- 3 tbsp olive oil
- 1 tsp cumin seeds
- Salt and freshly ground black pepper
- 2 tbsp butter
- 1 tbsp chopped fresh rosemary
- 1½ tbsp apricot jam

Follow these directions to prepare:

1. Heat oil in large skillet over medium-high heat. Add carrots and parsnips. Sprinkle with coarse kosher salt & pepper. Sauté until vegetables are beginning to brown at edges, about 12 minutes. DO AHEAD: *Can be made 1 day ahead. Cover and chill.*
2. Add butter, rosemary, and Apricot Jam to vegetables. Toss over medium heat until heated through and vegetables are glazed, about 5 minutes. Season to taste with more salt and pepper, if desired.

A favorite for any holiday, fig jam on a pita with fresh spinach and feta cheese, served with balsamic vinegar and fresh fruit. Light, memorable, beautiful.

DESSERTS

AUTUMN SPICE CAKE

Everyone has a favorite Autumn dessert, from apple pie and pumpkin pie, to cider doughnuts and chocolate fudge. This Autumn spice cake will join your favorites and perhaps surpass them as a staple to enjoy morning, afternoon, or as an evening snack.

A deliciously moist spice cake made with your favorite Autumn jam. Popular choices are Apple Jam, Raisin Jam, or Spiced Fig Jam. It is easy to make and memorable to serve. You might consider exploring new flavors by adding an orange marmalade glaze to top it off.

This recipe is very versatile. This autumn cake makes a memorable Bundt cake, drizzled with a delicate icing and sprinkled with powdered sugar. This recipe is also notable as a loaf served warm with butter and hot tea.

Perfectly paired with fresh whipped butter, and served warm, simply delightful.

The spice cake as a sheet cake or layer cake also makes a wonderful impression and is great for any occasion or given as a gift in a festive tin. Top your sheet cake with fresh whipped cream or layer with a beautiful butter cream and serve with pears and sharp cheddar cheese.

Enjoy this delicious cake as part of a casual afternoon repose with the addition of fresh oranges and hot brandy. It would be equally enjoyable with Orange Marmalade and an aged sipping bourbon. Perhaps a cup of hot cocoa, a chocolate peppermint stick and some fresh figs would better suit the cake on a snowy afternoon.

It's always a delightful surprise to find a friend bearing a lovely home-baked treat. Pair this simple delight with a jar of your favorite LunaGrown Jam, share your company and make someone smile.

A thoughtful and delicious way to say thank you.

OUR FAVORITE AUTUMN SPICE CAKE

INGREDIENTS

- 1 cup oil
- 1 cup sugar
- 3 eggs
- 1 tsp soda
- 2 cups flour
- 1 tsp nutmeg
- 1 tsp allspice
- 1 tsp cinnamon
- 1 tsp salt
- ½ cup buttermilk
- 1 tsp. vanilla
- 1 jar LunaGrown Fig, Apple or raisin Jam
- 1 cup chopped Walnuts or Pecans (optional)

INSTRUCTIONS

1. Heat oven to 325°.
2. Grease or spray with baking spray a 9 x 13 inch pan.
3. Combine flour, sugar, baking soda, salt, and spices in a large mixing bowl; add oil and beat well.
4. Add eggs and beat until well blended. Beat in buttermilk and vanilla.
5. Stir in preserves and chopped pecans (nuts optional).
6. Pour into the prepared baking pan; bake for 35 to 40 minutes, or until a toothpick or cake tester inserted into the cake comes out clean.

SWISS JELLY ROLL

Make a cake to delight all ages by filling it with strawberry or blueberry jam and soft ice cream. Roll, freeze, and serve.

A Swiss Jelly Roll with jam, marmalade, ice cream or whipped cream and fresh fruit makes an impression. There is just something fun about them. Jelly rolls are a wonderful creation made with a delicious sponge cake and all the imagination you can muster!

Interestingly, Swiss Jelly Rolls are not originally from Switzerland. It is a traditional German, Austrian, Hungarian type of cake.

The earliest published recipe known for a jelly roll is in the Northern Farmer, a journal published in Utica, New York, in December 1852. The recipe describes a modern "jelly roll" and reads: "Bake quick, and while hot spread with jelly. Roll carefully, and wrap it in a cloth. When cold cut in slices for the table."

Many diverse cultures have treats consisting of rolled cakes and fillings.

In Chinese bakeries the rolled cake can be found made with fillings that include chocolate, strawberry, coffee, orange or mango flavorings.

In a tiny village, in the south Indian state of Kerala, a special type of Swiss roll with pineapple jelly filling was developed by Kunju's cake shop started in 1931. In other Asian countries they flavor the Swiss roll with coconut (kaya), pandan, blueberry, strawberry and vanilla.

Many bakeries make the Swiss roll fresh daily and fill with butter cream, cheese or fruit jam. The Swiss roll is commonly sold by the slice for individual servings and not as a full roll.

Enjoy this Swiss Jelly (jam) roll! These make a great impression for any kind of special gathering – the spiral of color and texture lend a bit of visual whimsy. Swiss Jelly Rolls are great with tea, coffee, and a visit with a good friend.

SWISS JELLY ROLL

INGREDIENTS

- 4 eggs, separated
- ¾ cup sugar
- 1 tbsp vanilla
- ¾ cup cake flour, sifted
- ¾ tsp baking powder
- ¼ tsp salt

FILLING

- 9 ounces strawberry jam or lemon marmalade
- ¼ cup confectioners' sugar
- Whipped Cream

INSTRUCTIONS

1. Preheat oven to 400 degrees F.
2. In a small bowl beat egg whites until stiff but not dry and set aside. In another bowl, beat the egg yolks until light. Gradually add the sugar and vanilla, and mix well. Sift together the flour, baking powder, and salt. Add the sifted flour mixture to the egg yolk mixture. Fold in the egg whites into the egg mixture and pour the batter into a 15 by 10 by 1-inch jelly roll pan lined with waxed paper. Bake for 8 to 10 minutes or until the cake is golden.
3. Loosen edges of cake, invert cake onto a towel dusted with confectioners' sugar. Gently peel wax paper off cake. Trim ¼-inch of hard crust off each long side of the jelly roll cake. Begin with the narrow side and roll the cake and towel up together. Cool cake on rack, seam side down, for 10 to 15 minutes.
4. Once cake has cooled, gently unroll and spread cake with jam or jelly and re-roll. Sprinkle with confectioners' sugar or cover with whipped cream.

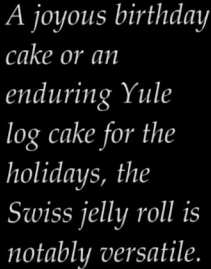

A joyous birthday cake or an enduring Yule log cake for the holidays, the Swiss jelly roll is notably versatile.

CRANBERRY BAKED APPLE

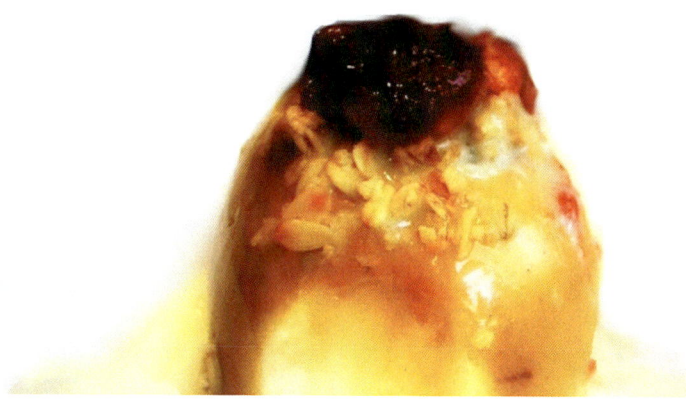

Cranberry Jam is a favored ingredient in many baked apple desserts. A local artisan was kind enough to share her recipe-noting that everyone has their own special way or creating baked apple for their family.

Here in New York's Hudson Valley there are an abundance of apples long after the harvest season is over. Favorite cooking apples are Honey Crisp, Galas and even Golden Delicious for both cooking and snacking.

Learning to make an old favorite is a simple joy that has been nearly forgotten. Baked apples are a tradition for many families, and each family seems to have their own take on this down-home dessert. For many the recipe is as simple as brown sugar, cinnamon, and raisins.

Some prefer to fill the baked apple with a combination of berries and nuts topped with vanilla cream or ice cream and brandy. This recipe is a combination of a classically filled baked apple with that of an apple dumpling. Enjoy the addition of a bit of caramel sauce and some pecans, or you may prefer a pat of butter and some apple brandy.

Baked Apple with Cranberry Jam

INGREDIENTS

- 4-6 medium apples we prefer Gala or Golden Delicious
- 1-9 ounce jar Cranberry Jam
- ½ cup flour
- ½ cup cinnamon and sugar
- Puff pastry
- Caramel sauce (optional)
- Walnuts, or Pecans, raisins (optional)

INSTRUCTIONS

1. Peel and core the apples leaving the bottom of the apple intact.
2. Combine cinnamon and sugar with your flour and roll apples in the mixture until well coated.
3. Fill the center of the apple with LunaGrown Cranberry Jam.
4. Roll out pastry dough and wrap apple pinching the dough at the top to create a seal.
5. Place apples in a 9 x 9 glass pan and put in the freezer for 10 minutes. (this will keep the pastry dough from sagging to the bottom of the apple during the baking process.
6. Heat oven to 375°. Cook apples for 25 - 35 minutes or until pastry is golden brown.
7. Top with warm caramel and chopped nuts if desired.

Cranberry Jam is endeared by many. This baked apple recipe is guaranteed to become a favorite and would make a great addition to a weekend breakfast.

When made in a decorative baking dish, baked apples make a nice warm gift for an old friend. The scent of delicious apple, and cranberry being baked together will warm your heart and delight your senses.

PROFITEROLES

"I don't know why people don't make these little devils more often."

The pastry for these takes about 10 minutes to create and they are so versatile. In the photo to the left, the profiterole is filled with sweetened cream cheese and blueberry jam. The possibilities are endless though.

Jam and cream cheese or jam and custard is the standard in many regions. Profiteroles are often used as a dessert or canapé at social functions.

By adjusting the size of your pastries you can adjust the fillings, from mini to full size. Mini profiteroles being served at parties and full size being served at meals or more intimate gatherings.

You might enjoy the following combinations:

- Crab meat with spinach and Chipotle Pepper Jam topped with a sour cream and chives sauce.

- Homemade ice cream with Blueberry Jam and coconut sauce

- Creamy raw milk cheese with Spice Fig Jam and a bittersweet chocolate sauce

- Chicken salad, feta cheese with Pineapple Jam

These would be a wonderful addition to any gathering filled with a soft goat cheese and some black currant jam. Imagine the astonished looks on your guests faces when you delight them with a puff filled with chicken and Swiss chard sautéed in Hot Pepper Jelly. Let your imagination run wild and enjoy this simple recipe.

PROFITEROLES

INGREDIENTS

- 1 cup water
- 1 stick butter (1/2 cup)
- 1 cup all purpose flour
- 1 good pinch of salt
- 1 cup eggs (4 large eggs)
- 1 tsp sugar

INSTRUCTIONS

1. Preheat oven 425F.
2. In a medium pot, bring the water and butter to a simmer on medium heat. Add the flour and with a wooden spoon or spatula, stir very quickly in one direction. Carefully watch and you'll see that the flour starts absorbing the liquid -- and a dough will form. Keep stirring to continue cooking the flour and cook off some of the water, another minute or two.
3. You can do the next step one of two ways:
4. Transfer the paste to the bowl of a standing mixer fitted with the paddle attachment or to a bowl if you're using a hand mixer.
5. If you want to mix the eggs directly into the dough in the pot, let it cool slightly, 4 or 5 minutes, or cool off the pan itself by running cold water over its base if you will be mixing the eggs in that pot. You don't want to cook the eggs too quickly.
6. If you do not allow some cooling time your eggs will cook into a scrambled mess.
7. Add the salt, sugar and the eggs one at a time mixing rapidly until each is combined into the paste. The paste will go from shiny to slippery to sticky as the egg is incorporated. The pâte a choux can be cooked immediately at this point or refrigerated for up to a day until ready to use.
8. Spoon the dough into a large gallon-sized plastic bag (or piping bag.) Use your hands to squeeze dough towards the bottom corner. With kitchen shears, snip off just the tippy tip of the bag, about ¼" of the tip. Pipe onto a baking sheet into little puffs, keeping the puffs 2-inches apart. With your finger, press down the peaks (as they can burn.) Bake at 425F for 10 minutes, then 350F for 18-30 minutes, depending on the size of your puffs.

Profiterole shells are very easy to make and can be filled to your desire. Try a Triple Cream Cheese, and chipotle jam topped with a bittersweet chocolate sauce.

COFFEE CAKE WITH FRESH BERRIES AND JAM

This simple coffee cake recipe has been a go to favorite for LunaGrown for some years now. It's simple, quick and so versatile.

INGREDIENTS

CRUMB TOPPING

- ½ cup sugar
- pinch salt
- 1½ cup all-purpose flour
- 1 stick butter, melted
- You may add spice or zest to your liking

CAKE

- 1 cup sugar
- ½ cup butter, softened
- 1 tsp vanilla extract
- 2 large eggs
- 2 cups all-purpose flour
- 1 tsp baking powder
- ½ tsp baking soda
- ½ tsp salt
- 1 buttermilk
- 1 cup fresh berries
- 1 jar LunaGrown Jam or Marmalade

INSTRUCTIONS

FOR CRUMB TOPPING

1. In a medium bowl, stir together dry topping ingredients until combined, then stir in melted butter until damp crumbs are formed and the mixture sticks together into chunks when you squeeze it between your fingers. Set aside.

FOR CAKE

1. Preheat oven to 350F and line a 10" x 8" square pan with parchment paper and set aside.
2. In a large bowl, cream together sugar and butter until light and fluffy. Beat in vanilla, followed by the eggs, adding them one at a time until mixture is smooth.
3. In a medium bowl, whisk together flour, baking powder, baking soda and salt. Add to sugar mixture, alternating with buttermilk in two or three additions, until well blended.
4. Add fresh berries and fold in by hand.
5. Batter will be quite thick. Spread evenly into prepared pan.
6. Stir jam in a small bowl until smooth and drop by spoonfuls onto the cake batter. Gently swirl through with a knife. Top with crumb mixture, clumping it by squeezing it between your fingers while you work and spreading it into as even a layer as possible.
7. Bake for 25-35 minutes or until toothpick inserted into the center comes out clean.
8. Cool on a wire rack for at least 30 minutes before slicing.

It is a welcome and thoughtful addition to any breakfast or brunch, or a light afternoon snack that is just so refreshing. What makes this cake truly your own is your favorite flavor of jam swirled into the batter before baking.

Choose your favorite berries or finely chopped fruit to complement your jam choice. You may also choose to add some nuts or raisins. Pick your favorite jam to incorporate and enjoy!

Tea time, coffee time, break time, a great replacement for prepackaged snack cakes.

THE FARMGIRL'S JAM CRUMBLE BARS

This is a classic favorite for many jam lovers. It's quick and easy to create and is always a big hit at any social event. What makes it even nicer is its versatility. Choose your favorite jam and then take it a step or two further.

Utilize oatmeal, pecans, chocolate chips, coconut, raisins, peanut butter chips or any combination you feel your jam might lead you to consider. Once cut into serving portions, you may choose to frost these with icing.

This version of jam crumble bars has been perfected by a local artisan, it is lower in sugar than most recipes. This recipe may be cut in half if you are not offering to a large crowd, but perhaps creating for a small gathering or for your home.

These bars also freeze nicely so that you may create them ahead of time, remember to cook them prior to freezing.

If you prefer, you may substitute 1/2 cup of flour with 1/2 cup of rolled oats. Please <u>do not </u>use instant oats - you will be very disappointed!

INGREDIENTS

- 3 cups all purpose flour
- ⅓ cup + 2 tbsp white sugar
- ¼ cup + 2 tbsp brown sugar
- 1½ tsp baking powder
- ½ tsp salt (do not omit)
- 3 sticks COLD butter, unsalted and cut into bits
- 1½ tsp vanilla extract
- 2 egg yolks
- 9 oz LunaGrown Jam

INSTRUCTIONS

1. Combine flour, sugars baking powder and salt in bowl of food processor. Pulse a few times until all dry ingredients are evenly distributed.
2. Add butter and pulse again until coarse crumbs form. Add extract and egg yolks then pulse a few more times until all ingredients combine into big hunks of beautiful dough.
3. Remove ¾ cup of dough and set aside. Pour remainder of dough into buttered 12 x 8 pan (1/4-sheet size) and press down into an even layer with just a small rim rising around the edges.
4. Spread the unbaked crust with your favorite LunaGrown Jam then sprinkle the reserved crumbs evenly over the top.
5. If you are adding additional items such as nuts, dried fruits, or chocolate chips, combine about ½ to ¾ cup to the crumbs you are using for the top layer. Avoid adding these to the bottom crust layer as they may stick to the bottom of the pan.
6. Bake this in a preheated 350° oven for 30 minutes. I like to give mine a 180-degree turn about halfway through cooking so it cooks evenly. My oven isn't very consistent.
7. Remove from oven and cool on wire rack until completely cool. Store for a week or more well-wrapped in plastic wrap or a tightly closed container.
8. If you would like to whip some icing up for your Jam Crumble Bars, a teaspoon of butter, ¼ cup of milk, and powdered sugar to the consistency you are looking for will do the trick! You may add a little vanilla, or some orange zest to give your treat a personal touch. We won't tell your secret!

The farm girl creates these jam crumble bars for large events during the holiday season. They have become a requested community favorite.

KEY LIME CHEESECAKE WITH STRAWBERRY JAM

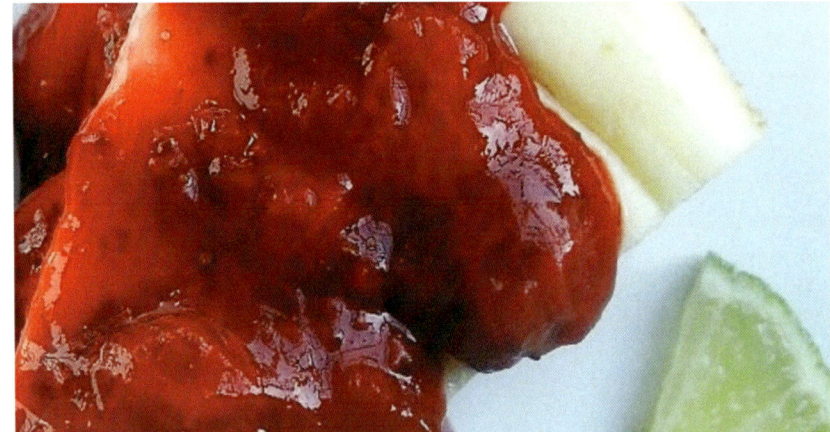

Strawberry jam, Mango jam, Pineapple jam, all make a standout topping for this key lime cheesecake. A tropical reminder of an indulgent summer.

Summertime is perfect for anything lime, and authentic key limes are especially desired for their distinctive sweet-tart Floridian flavor.

The combination of key limes and rich cream cheese is harmonious. Top that off with strawberry jam and you have the perfect triple play. Key limes and strawberry all in one beautiful fruitful dessert.

Key lime cheesecake makes a beautiful gift, and is impressive to serve when entertaining guests at home. Whether for a holiday gathering or just an afternoon of tea or martinis by the pool, this cheesecake will certainly be remembered.

When approaching cheesecake creation it's important to have the correct pan and follow the directions. Cheese cakes are fairly easy to create, however if this is your first attempt make sure to use the appropriate measuring tools and ingredients. You will be delighted with the results!

INGREDIENTS

LIME CUSTARD

- 6 large egg yolks (room temp)
- ¾ cup sugar
- 6 tablespoons fresh Key lime juice or regular lime juice
- 1 tsp grated Key lime peel or regular lime peel

CRUST

- 1¾ cups graham cracker crumbs (about 12 whole graham crackers)
- ¼ cup sugar
- ½ tsp salt
- ½ cup (1 stick) unsalted butter, melted

FILLING

- 2 (8 ounce) packages cream cheese, room temperature
- ⅔ cup plus 3 tablespoons sugar
- 2 large eggs
- 3 tbsp fresh Key lime juice or regular lime juice
- 1 tbsp grated Key lime peel or regular lime peel
- 1 16-ounce container sour cream
- Thin lime slices

Serve this cheesecake with additional slices of key lime, fresh strawberries, fresh whipped cream and some coconut and chocolate shavings for an amazing visual impact. This key lime cheesecake is also excellent with mango jam, pineapple jam, and even with lemon or lime marmalades.

A beautiful dessert you will enjoy making and sharing for years to come. Guaranteed a family favorite.

INSTRUCTIONS

FOR LIME CUSTARD:

1. Whisk all ingredients in heavy small saucepan over medium heat until custard thickens and boils for 30 seconds, about 8 minutes. Cool to room temperature, stirring occasionally (mixture will thicken).

FOR CRUST:

1. Preheat oven to 350°F. Wrap 3 layers of foil around outside of 8- to 8½-inch-diameter springform pan with 3-inch-high sides. Butter pan. Stir first 3 ingredients to blend in medium bowl. Mix in butter until moistened.
2. Press crumb mixture evenly onto bottom and 1½ inches up sides of prepared pan. Bake just until set, about 5 minutes. Cool completely. Maintain oven temperature.

FOR FILLING:

1. Place cream cheese, ⅔ cup sugar, eggs, lime juice, and lime peel in processor; blend well.
2. Spoon custard into crust; smooth top. Carefully spoon filling over the custard. Set cheesecake in large baking pan. Add enough hot water to baking pan to come 1 inch up sides of cheesecake pan. Bake until almost set but not puffed and center moves slightly when pan is gently shaken, about 45 minutes.
3. Meanwhile, stir sour cream and remaining 3 tablespoons sugar in medium bowl to blend.
4. Carefully spoon sour cream mixture over hot cheesecake; smooth top. Bake until topping sets, about 10 minutes. Cool 10 minutes. Run knife around sides of pan to loosen.
5. Cool cheesecake completely. Cover and refrigerate overnight. Do ahead Can be made 2 days ahead. Keep refrigerated. Release pan sides from cheesecake; transfer to platter. Garnish with lime slices, LunaGrown Strawberry Jam and serve.

With a bit of patience a velvety cheesecake can be easily created for most any occasion.

CHEESECAKE MINIS WITH LUNAGROWN JAM

Cheesecake minis are great for social gatherings and events. These are easy to make, beautiful to serve and make a tasteful impact.

This recipe for mini cheesecakes is exceptionally simple to make, these little treats are very tasty, and they make a big impact when given as a gift or at any kind of social event. Top with a bit of your favorite jam, perhaps some crushed nuts, or shredded chocolate and you have become the neighborhood gourmet!

This recipe is intended to be used for creating these cheesecake mini's, not a full cheesecake in a spring pan. Anyone who owns a spring pan already has a favorite recipe. The corn starch may be omitted, however, your cheesecakes will be less creamy.

When it comes to the right jam to choose, we can only suggest that you pick a favorite! You can't go wrong here. If these are to be served as part of dinner or in between courses rather than as a dessert, we would suggest considering a marmalade to help cleanse the palate

CHEESECAKE MINI'S

INGREDIENTS

Cheesecake

- 2 - 8 ounce packages cream cheese (room temp)
- ½ cup of sugar
- ½ tbsp corn starch
- dash salt
- ¼ cup sour cream
- dash lemon juice
- 1 tsp vanilla
- 1 large egg
- 1 egg yolk

Crust

- ½ stick butter (melted)
- 6 tbsp graham cracker crumbs or crushed pecan sandies

INSTRUCTIONS

1. In a food processor place cream cheese and sugar. pulse together until well combined.
2. Add sour cream and eggs. pulse until ingredients are smooth.
3. Add balance of ingredients: cornstarch, salt, lemon, and vanilla. Process until mixture is that of thick creamy pancake batter (it will be a bit thicker but smooth)
4. Pre-heat oven to 350°
5. Create crust by adding gram cracker crumbs to melted butter.
6. Place paper liners in a mini muffin pan and pat a small bit of gram cracker crust in the bottom of each cup.
7. Pour batter into cups just about to the top. These will rise when cooking and then fall once completely cooled.
8. Bake for appx 20 minutes or until the center is bouncy when you tap it.
9. Allow to cool for at least 2 hours (this is very important). then top with your favorite jam and serve.

Recipe creates 24-36 mini cheesecakes (using a mini muffin pan) 12-16 in a standard size muffin pan.

Any confection can be versatile, a touch of jam can make the difference in texture, flavor, and appearance. Blueberry jam with whipped cream, verses Chipotle jam with bittersweet chocolate pieces. Both amazing, yet offering completely different flavor nuances.

BANANA CAKE WITH HONEY MANGO JAM

The addition of Mango jam to this cake offers a slight hit of mango flavor while ensuring the cake remains moist with little effort. Excellent served with a pat of butter.

It's that time when bananas are on sale and you can't help but buy a whole bunch of green ones thinking you will eat most of them before they start to turn brown. Then they turn brown.

If you are wise, you sliced and froze them. Frozen bananas are a perfect addition to morning smoothies or protein shakes. Of course there's always banana cream pie, or caramelized banana cheesecake, or the baked chocolate banana French toast. But not for many of us.

There is nothing nicer on a cold day, when you long for something tropical and can't get away to that island paradise. Banana Cake with Honey Mango jam sounds great! Topped with organic toasted coconut flakes, this would be great with some hot tea, even better with a coconut mango martini.

This recipe is low in sugar so it is best served with a jar of pineapple jam and some homemade whipped cream or butter. It is a delightful addition to your breakfast, toasted or plain, perhaps served with some yogurt and granola.

BANANA CAKE WITH LUNAGROWN HONEY MANGO JAM

INGREDIENTS

- 1 cup sugar
- ½ cup butter softened
- 2 eggs
- 2 large very ripe bananas
- ½ cup buttermilk
- 1 tbsp Vanilla
- 2½ cups flour
- 1 tsp baking soda
- 1 tsp salt
- 1 9oz jar LunaGrown Mango Jam
- 1 cup nuts (optional)

INSTRUCTIONS

1. Pre-heat oven to 350°, grease and flour standard Bundt pan.
2. Mix sugar and butter in large bowl. Stir in eggs until well blended. Add bananas, buttermilk and vanilla. Beat until smooth.
3. Stir in flour, baking soda and salt just until moistened. Stir in nuts. Pour into greased and floured Bundt pan
4. Bake for hr and min or until tooth pic inserted comes out clean. Allow cake to cool for 10 minutes then flip pan and allow cake to rest on serving plate until cool enough to frost.
5. Top with warm icing and toasted coconut, serve with LunaGrown Pineapple Jam and fresh butter.

MARMALADE GLAZE FOR AN ELEGANT FLAIR

Glazes are one of the easiest, and most impactful ways to increase the visible appeal of your confection, while adding a note flavor.

There are so many wonderful things to do with a good marmalade. Marmalade is one spread enjoyable specifically on tea biscuits or a nice English muffin. However its applications are as versatile as any jam. A marmalade glaze for any pound cake pushes the limits of flavor.

The marmalade glaze can also be utilized on grilled salmon, chicken wings, even meatloaf. The hint of flavor added by utilizing one of LunaGrown's signature marmalade's is enlightening.

Employ Orange Marmalade or Lemon Lavender Marmalade to create a marmalade glaze that will tantalize your palate!

Be creative and explore other spices when creating your glaze such as hot pepper, fresh cilantro or fresh chives. The addition of garden fresh herbs blend very nicely and with a variety of marmalades, allowing you to create for the more refined diner. The possibilities are endless.

POUND CAKE WITH MARMALADE GLAZE

INGREDIENTS

- 1½ cups all purpose flour
- 2 tsp baking powder
- ¼ tsp salt
- 1 cup plain whole-milk yogurt
- 1 cup sugar
- 3 large eggs
- 1 tbsp marmalade
- ¼ tsp vanilla extract
- ½ cup melted butter
- ¼ cup lemon, orange, or grapefruit marmalade (for glaze)
- 1 tsp water

INSTRUCTIONS

1. Position rack in center of oven and preheat to 350°F.
2. Generously butter 8½x4½x2½-inch metal loaf pan.
3. Sift flour, baking powder, and salt into medium bowl. Combine yogurt, sugar, eggs, marmalade, and vanilla in large bowl; whisk until well blended.
4. Gradually whisk in dry ingredients. Using rubber spatula, fold in melted butter. Transfer batter to prepared pan. Place pan on baking sheet.
5. Place cake on baking sheet in oven and bake until cake begins to pull away from sides of pan and tester inserted into center comes out clean, about 50 minutes.
6. Cool cake in pan on rack 5 minutes. Cut around pan sides to loosen cake. Turn cake out onto rack. Turn cake upright on rack and cool completely.
7. Stir marmalade and 1 teaspoon water in small saucepan over medium heat until marmalade melts. Brush hot mixture over top of cake. Let glaze cool and set. Cut cake crosswise into slices.

JAM FILLED COFFEE CAKE

Jam filled coffee cake is the jam maker's go to recipe for leaving an especially positive impression. The added jam, or marmalade, and sour cream create a moist cake that offers layers of flavor, yet is not overwhelmingly sweet.

This coffee cake makes a perfect gift, is beautiful to serve at any social gathering and imparts respect for both tradition and whimsy. A grand opportunity to experience your favorite jam in a new way.

CAKE

- 1 cup sugar
- ½ cup butter, softened
- 1 tsp vanilla extract
- 2 large eggs
- 2 cups all-purpose flour
- 1 tsp baking powder
- ½ tsp baking soda
- ½ tsp salt
- 1 cup sour cream (light is fine)
- 1 9 ounce jar of your favorite jam (

CRUMB TOPPING

- ¼ cup brown sugar
- ¼ cup sugar
- 1 tsp cinnamon
- pinch salt
- 1 cup plus 2 tablespoons all-purpose flour
- ⅓ cup butter, melted

FROSTING

- 3 tbsp butter melted
- 1 cup powder sugar
- 2 tbsp maple syrup
- ¼ tsp cinnamon

INSTRUCTIONS

FOR CRUMB TOPPING

1. In a medium bowl, stir together dry topping ingredients until combined, then stir in melted butter until damp crumbs are formed and the mixture sticks together into chunks when you squeeze it between your fingers. Set aside.

FOR CAKE

1. Preheat oven to 350°. Grease and flour a 9 x 13" glass pan and set aside.
2. In a large bowl, cream together sugar and butter until light and fluffy. Beat in vanilla, followed by the eggs, adding them one at a time until mixture is smooth.
3. In a medium bowl, whisk together flour, baking powder, baking soda and salt. Add to sugar mixture, alternating with sour cream in two or three additions, until well blended. Batter will be quite thick. Spread evenly into prepared pan.
4. Stir jam in a small bowl until smooth and drop by spoonfuls onto the cake batter. Gently swirl through with a knife. Top with crumb mixture, clumping it by squeezing it between your fingers while you work and spreading it into as even a layer as possible.
5. Bake for 20-25 minutes. Remove from oven, add crumb topping and return to oven for 20-25 minutes longer. Cool for at least 60 minutes before slicing. Cake will be warm.
6. Serves 15-24 (depending on how you slice it)
7. Allow cake to completely cool before icing.

COOKIES

JAM FILLED SPRITZ COOKIES

Spritz cookies are a multi generational favorite with flavor variations as diverse as the holidays they represent. This basic recipe for Spritz cookies is perfect for using in a cookie gun or a pastry bad to create the shapes you desire.

Choose a favorite jam and enjoy. These will soften up hours after the jam has been added. Perfect with tea and light fare. A beautiful gift!

INGREDIENTS

- ½ cup (1 stick) Butter
- ½ cup shortening
- ¾ cup of sugar
- 1 egg yolk (toss the white)
- 2 tsp vanilla flavoring
- 1 tsp almond flavoring
- 2½ cups white all purpose flour
- ¼ tsp salt

INSTRUCTIONS

1. Combine butter, shortening, sugar, egg, and flavorings in a bowl and whip together. Make certain these ingredients are well combined and creamed.
2. Add flour and salt. Mix well. This dough should easily pull away from the sides of your bowl.
3. Roll dough into a 'log' shape and insert into your cookie press or pastry bag and press out your shapes. Cooler dough works best, very cold dough can be challenging and warm dough will just make a mess.
4. Bake at 350° for 10 minutes. Make certain your oven is preheated!
5. Once the cookies have baked and cooled, sandwich ½ teaspoon of LunaGrown jam between two cookies. Place on a drying rack or flat surface overnight.
6. Decorate the following day

BLEEDING ZOMBIE FINGER COOKIES

A favorite way to employ an open jar of jam is finger dipping, with these fun Halloween zombie finger cookies. Children and adults will squeal with delight as they dip these cookie fingers into delicious jam "blood".

The creativity that goes with Halloween is admirable and these zombie cookie fingers are no exception. Great for both children's and adult parties alike. These Bleeding Zombie Finger Cookies are a wonderful way to get into the creepy spirit no matter how you intend on celebrating.

Luckily these take very little time to make and are a huge impact at gatherings. Children are amazed at the Zombie fingers and delight in eating them! As for adults, well some like giving the finger and what a nice way of doing so by offering up a Bleeding Zombie Finger Cookie.

One of the nice things about this recipe is it can also be made into Skeleton Bones for dipping in your favorite Zombie Jam blood. No one knows for sure what color Zombie blood is or what it tastes like so you can serve these up with any of your favorite Jams.

BLEEDING ZOMBIE FINGER COOKIES

INGREDIENTS

- 1⅛ cups Unsalted butter
- 1½ cups Sugar
- ¾ tsp salt
- 1 large egg
- ¼ cup Whole milk
- 1 tsp Vanilla
- 1 tbsp Lemon zest,
- 4¼ cups Cake flour
- 1¼ tbsp Baking powder
- Whole almonds
- Raspberry or Strawberry Jam

INSTRUCTIONS

1. Preheat oven to 350 F.
2. Cream the butter, sugar and salt in an electric mixer with a paddle attachment until light and fluffy.
3. Add the egg, then the milk, vanilla and zest. Scrape down the sides of the bowl with a rubber spatula and mix again.
4. Sift together flour and baking powder. Add dry mixture to wet mixture and blend just until combined.
5. Wrap dough in plastic wrap and chill until firm.
6. Take about 2 to 3 tablespoons of dough per finger. Roll each into a ball, then a log, and shape into a finger with knuckle marks. Make an indent at one end for fingernail, smear some raspberry jam into it and place whole almond in the indent. Bake for 8 to 10 minutes. You might need to add more jam once cooled for a bloodied look.

SAY I LOVE YOU WITH JAM FILLED COOKIES

A Valentine's Day favorite from The Farm Girl. She shares one of her favorite treats for the holiday. Simple and elegant, and more importantly, straight from the heart!

If you can give nothing more than a smile on Valentines day, then you've just made the world a bit more beautiful! The Farm Girl tells us that these are wonderful for classroom parties! That is if you live in an area of the country that still allows such fanciful events!

Children and adults will love the memorable decorations you create. For many, jam filled beats the frosted decorations anytime. Why not mix it up!

A perfect way to celebrate at the office, these cookies also make a wonderful homemade gift for a close friend. They are, quite possibly, the best midnight snack to follow that romantic interlude! No matter how you choose to celebrate Valentine's day, these cookies are guaranteed to leave a sweet memory in someone's heart.

You may add ¼ cup of cocoa to this recipe for a light chocolate cookie. Splitting the batch, one with cocoa and one without, will give you a larger choice of flavor combinations.

The combination of chocolate or vanilla with raspberry or blueberry jam is impressive consider taking it up a notch by creating a sweet and spicy chocolate or vanilla Chipotle jelly filled cookie. Now there's a warm treat for your valentine.

These jam and jelly filled cookies are wonderful served with some triple cream cheese, fresh fruit and a bottle of wine.

FAVORITE ROLL-OUT COOKIE DOUGH

INGREDIENTS

- 1 cup (2 sticks) unsalted butter, softened
- 1½ cups granulated sugar
- 1 egg
- 1½ tsp vanilla extract
- ½ tsp almond extract
- 2¾ cups all-purpose flour
- 1 tsp baking powder
- 1 tsp salt

INSTRUCTIONS

1. Preheat oven to 350ºF.
2. In large bowl, beat butter and sugar with electric mixer until light and fluffy. Beat in egg and extracts. Mix flour, baking powder and salt; add to butter mixture 1 cup at a time, mixing after each addition. Do not chill dough. Divide dough into 2 balls.
3. On floured surface, roll each ball into a circle approximately ½ in. diameter x ⅛ in. thick. Dip cookie cutter in flour before each use. Bake cookies on ungreased cookie sheet 8-11 minutes or until cookies are lightly browned.
4. Once cookies are cooled sandwich with jam and allow to sit overnight. Decorate with frosting or powdered sugar a few hours prior to serving.

THUMBPRINT SUGAR COOKIES

INGREDIENTS

- 1 cup butter or shortening
- 2 egg
- 1 cup sugar
- 3 cups flour
- 1 tsp baking soda
- 2 tsp baking powder
- 1 tsp vanilla
- 1 tsp nutmeg

INSTRUCTIONS

1. Preheat oven to 350 degrees.
2. Whisk the flour, baking soda, salt and nutmeg together in a bowl.
3. In another bowl, whip the butter and the sugar until fluffy, about 5 minutes. Beat in the egg and vanilla until just combined. Add the dry ingredients until dough reaches a creamy consistency.
4. Refrigerate covered at least 1 hour or overnight.
5. Scoop the dough into 1-inch balls with a cookie or ice cream scoop and roll in sugar. Place about 2-inches apart on the baking sheets. Press a thumbprint into the center of each ball, about ½-inch deep. Fill each indentation with about ¾ teaspoon jam.
6. Bake cookies until the edges are golden, about 15 minutes. Cool cookies on the baking sheets. Serve.
7. Store cookies in a tightly sealed container for up to 5 days.

PEANUT BUTTER COOKIES AND GRAPE JELLY

Take peanut butter and jelly to a new level. Serve or sandwich with Grape Jelly.

These are the jam maker's, favorite of all time, peanut butter cookies. They are so good we suggest making a double batch and freezing some for later. It is very easy to eat an entire batch of these cookies in one sitting. So be warned!

The pairing of Grape Jelly with these peanut butter cookies is a match made on the counter top! Great for sunny days, or rainy days. Guaranteed to create smiles.

You may choose your favorite nut butter, and even create these with smooth or chunky butter. These peanut butter cookies bake up beautifully soft and stay that way!

Combined with a jar of LunaGrown NY Grape Jelly these make a perfect gift. A thoughtful way to say thank you for a kindness someone has show you. A favorite with old and young alike!

SOFT PEANUT BUTTER COOKIES

INGREDIENTS

- 1 cup peanut butter (or your favorite nut butter)
- 1 cup brown sugar
- 1 cup white sugar
- 1 stick butter
- ½ cup shortening
- 2 eggs
- 1 tsp baking soda
- 1 tsp baking powder
- 1 tbsp vanilla
- 2½ cups flour

INSTRUCTIONS

1. Cream together, butter, shortening, nut butter, and sugars
2. Add eggs one at a time
3. Add baking powder, soda and vanilla, continue to mix well
4. Add flour and beat until creamy.
5. Place covered in refrigerator for 30 minutes
6. Using a melon baller, or small spoon, create balls and roll in sugar if desired
7. Place on cookie sheet and create cris cross with fork
8. Bake for 10-15 minutes at 350°
9. Allow to cool on cooling rack, serve with your favorite jelly

ADDITIONAL IDEAS

1. Preserves make a great crepe filling, raspberry crepes with whipped cream anyone?
2. Swirl jams, or marmalade into plain yogurt (or applesauce!) for a custom flavor
3. Use jam or jelly as a glaze on a fresh fruit tart,
4. Mix jam with cream cheese and use as a filling for stuffed French toast
5. Glaze a ham with pineapple and apricot jams
6. Make jam oatmeal crumb bars
7. Spoon warm jam over ice cream, pair with a brownie or sponge cake, and top with chopped nuts and whipped cream
8. Use jam to top off a plain cheesecake
9. Mix Jam with vanilla frosting for a great way to liven up plain yellow cake
10. Try a sweet and spicy hot wing sauce, pineapple jam and add fresh minced jalapeño pepper for a spicy sweet sauce that's delicious on chicken wings.
11. Make berry lemonade
12. Use a spoonful or two of your favorite jam in a fruit smoothie to add sweetness and flavor
13. Use a bit of jam to fill a cupcake (cut out a round peg from the top, fill with jam, replace the cake, and frost for a sweet surprise)
14. Make baked brie appetizer
15. Peanut butter and jelly sandwiches
16. Spoon warm Jam over pancakes
17. Fill a macaroon with jam
18. If you're running low on fruit for mixed berry Mojitos, add a bit of blackberry or raspberry jam and omit the sugar
19. Make a fruity vinaigrette
20. Try a jam flavored cocktail

A good jam or marmalade can be a versatile addition to any meal or delight you can dream up. It's time to enjoy!

21. Fill a kolache, empanada, turnover, or Danish with jam.

22. Hot jam breakfast sandwiches

23. Jelly doughnuts anyone?

24. Make thumb print cookies

25. Homemade pop tarts are gaining popularity

26. Add a tablespoon of hot pepper jelly to stir fry just before serving

27. Make sweet jam BBQ sauce, combine 2 parts jam and 1 part BBQ sauce.

28. How about some fruity, frothy punch?

29. Jam filled chocolate truffles

30. Hide a layer of jam in a meringue pie, how about raspberry or strawberry with lemon meringue? (spread the jam on the pre-baked crust, freeze for a few minutes to set the jam and then add filling) ooh or swirl blackberry jam into key lime pie! how gorgeous would that be?

31. Try this devilish steak sauce

32. Make fancy flavored butter or cream cheese (2 parts room temperature butter with 1 part preserves, beat until thoroughly combined, chill if desired)

33. How about some spicy sweet Jezebel sauce?

34. Make a jam cake

35. Bake a bit of jam into muffins,

36. Turn drippings from pork or chicken into a delicious pan sauce with a cup of jam and a teaspoon of balsamic vinegar (try pineapple or strawberry jam, season with salt & pepper to taste)

37. Fold in ½ cup of jam into your favorite brownie mix for a new twist on the traditional

38. Hot pepper jelly spooned over a block of cream cheese and served with crackers is always a hit

39. Make sweet & sour sauce with plum jam

40. Spoon your favorite jam over baked apples or pears

41. Make a fresh fruit pizza, use a bit of jam for the sauce, add fruit and sprinkle with ricotta or bits of cream cheese, bake!

42. Lil' smokies swimming in equal parts warm grape jelly and chili sauce, strange but good

43. Have a tea party, serve your favorite tea blends, crumpets, and an assortment of preserves

44. Have a tasting party, put out a cheese plate with jam pairings, crackers, and wine

45. How about a grilled cheese with hot pepper jelly?

46. Combine hot pepper jelly with a bit of mayo and horseradish for a unique sandwich spread

47. Add preserves to a sweet noodle kugel

48. Make chicken tagine

49. Thin jam with a little water and warm to make a syrup, poke holes in a still warm cake, pour syrup over the top to infuse the cake with flavor

50. Try an orange marmalade ale

51. Fold preserves into fruit fluff desserts

52. Layer preserves in a trifle with fresh fruit, pudding, and whipped cream

53. Oh yeah, and you can spread it on toast!

QUICK REFERENCE

Here you find quick ideas utilizing Jam, Jelly or Marmalade by variety. These are suggestions. Some of the recipes you may find herein, some you may not, but you will have some ideas for additional usage of your favorite Jam, Jelly, or Marmalade. This reference is based on the varieties offered by LunaGrown Jam.

TRADITIONAL JAMS

- Apricot Jam
  - Filling in cookies
  - Crepes
  - Add in sauté
- Apple Jam
  - Pastry filling
  - Side condiment with poultry
  - Use in oatmeal or quinoa
- Blackberry Jam
  - Serve with ice cream
  - Breakfast with a triple cream cheese
  - In a margarita
- Wild Blueberry Jam
  - Serve with artisan bread and wine
  - Whip with ricotta cheese for pastry
  - Add to yogurt parfait
- Mango Jam
  - Excellent served with grilled salmon
  - Use in sauté
  - Add to summer cocktails
- Pear Jam
  - Perfect for cheese and wine pairing
  - Served with warm brandy
  - As a warmed side with roasted meats
- Plum Jam
  - Pastry filling or Profiteroles
  - Served with poultry or game birds
  - As a dipping sauce for biscotti
- Raspberry Jam
  - Cookie filling
  - Serve with ice cream
  - Ingredient in summer cocktail (think martini)
- Strawberry Jam
  - Serve with ice cream
  - Stir into cottage cheese
  - On shortcake

CONTINUING QUICK IDEAS BASED ON LUNAGROWN VARIETIES.

MARMALADES

- Pineapple Jam
    - As a BBQ sauce or side
    - Added to cottage or ricotta cheese
    - On a turkey sandwich
- Lemon Marmalade with Lavender *
    - Served in ice water on a hot day
    - Excellent in a martini
    - With steak fish such as tuna or shark
- Lime Marmalade
    - A wonderful glaze
    - Serve with corn chips and salsa
    - A nice addition to corn salsa
- Blood Orange Marmalade with Raspberries
    - Pairing with chocolates and fine cheese
    - Serve with fruit and nut breads
    - Alternative in a whiskey sour
- Orange Marmalade with Hawaiian Ginger *
    - Serve on French toast
    - With fish such as monk, cod or halibut
    - Paired with a sharp cheddar cheese

JELLIES

- Candy Apple Jelly
    - As a cookie filling
    - A beautiful glaze for pastry
    - On hot biscuits
- Chipotle Pepper Jelly
    - With cream cheese as a profiterole filling
    - Over ice cream with chocolate sauce
    - Sautee with vegetables and greens serve with rice
- New York Grape Jelly
    - With meatballs and lil smokies
    - PBJ on artisan bread
    - As a side with smoked meats
- Elderberry Jelly
    - With hot tea
    - Paired with a hard cheese such as Pecorino or Grana
    - Stirred into a cocktail

CONTINUING QUICK IDEAS BASED ON LUNAGROWN VARIETIES.

SIGNATURE JAMS

- Rica Barreja Jam (LunaGrown's Own Rich Blend)
    - With a spoon
- Cranberry Jam
    - As a pastry filling
    - With sharp cheddar cheese
    - With poultry
- Razzleberry Jam
    - As a cookie filling
    - Served with pork roasts
    - Combined with mustard on sandwiches
- Spiced Fig Jam
    - Serve with warm brandy
    - As a spread with meats and cheese
    - Pastry filling
- Cinnamon Raisin Jam
    - Pastry filling
    - Goat cheese crostini
    - With duck
- Honey Peach with Cherry
    - In a stir fry
    - With smoked meats
    - Belgian waffle with fresh fruits

COUNTRY TRADITIONAL JAMS

- Black Currant Jam
    - With game meats
    - Serve with tea and cake
    - Pan fish such as trout
- Green Tomato Jam
    - Serve with cheese
    - On Johnny cakes
    - Stuffed in seasonal squash
- Red Tomato Jam
    - On artisan grilled cheese sandwich
    - With roast beef
    - In a Bloody Mary